[COMPOSITION]

4TH EDITION

M. Smith-Autard

A & C Black

To Jason and Ryan

Fourth edition 2000
Third edition 1996
Second edition 1992
A & C Black (Publishers) Limited
35 Bedford Row, London WC1R 4JH

ISBN 0–7136–5457–0

Originally published 1976
by Lepus Books
© 1976 Lepus Books
(An associate member company of Henry Kimpton Ltd)

A CIP catalogue record for this book is available
from the British Library.

Typeset in 10 on 11½ pt Baskerville
by Florence Production Ltd, Stoodleigh, Devon
Printed in Great Britain by Biddles Ltd, Guildford, Surrey

CONTENTS

PREFACE

In the arts, to compose is to create – to make something which, for each particular artist, has not been in existence before. Artists who attain the highest peaks of perfection in composition – dance: the choreographer, music: the composer, art: the painter or sculptor, drama: the dramatist or playwright, literature: the poet or novelist – are inspired people of imagination and vision. The few who reach these heights of artistry are those with outstanding gifts and skills, and who, through many years of diligent and perceptive study, have mastered their craft so completely that they have no need to analyse the 'rules' when they become inspired to create 'something' which, in its finished form, is unique.

If we are realistic and honest with ourselves, the majority of us know that our talent, in the particular art in which we have chosen to be involved, may have many limitations when compared with those who are truly great. This is not to suggest that we under-estimate ourselves, but that self-assessment of our own ability is very important as it guards us from becoming pretentious in attempting what is beyond our skill.

The challenge to those who teach through an art is to encourage and guide students towards fulfilling their potential. During the process, the teacher and the taught may derive encouragement and inspiration from each other as well as from those who have been recognised as especially talented.

Although the term 'choreography' is commonly used to describe the activity of composing dances, the title of this book has been retained as *Dance Composition* because it focuses almost exclusively on the content and form of dances rather than on all aspects of choreography including themes, music or sound, design and lighting. Here dance composition is considered as a craft from the point of view of students and young teachers who are faced with the task of composing dances, and encouraging others to do the same. Many find difficulty in this creative aspect of the art of dance, often through lack of confidence due to insufficient knowledge of the guidelines. But what are the guidelines or 'rules' which become so absorbed and reflected in the works of those who have mastered the craft of their art? This book attempts to answer this question.

Acknowledgements

My thanks to Gordon Curl, Sarah Stevens and Brigitte Boast who took the time and trouble within their own busy schedules to read and comment on the two chapters added in the 3rd edition: *Methods of Construction 7 – Improvisation in the Process of Composition,* and *Methods of Construction 8 – Alternative and Experimental Approaches in Dance Composition.*

For this 4th edition I thank Jim Schofield, my partner in Bedford Interactive Research, whose innovative and inspiring ideas have advanced and enhanced the teaching of dance composition through the use of multimedia. Section 3, now entitled *Resource-based Teaching/Learning of Dance Composition and New Technologies,* has been re-written to reflect the new and exciting possibilities offered through the use of technology – exposing as it does, a whole range of teaching/learning activities derived from the study of a professionally choreographed dance work. Our work to author a CD resource pack featuring the Ludus Dance Company's *Wild Child* (1999), has led to fresh approaches in the use of resources in teaching/learning dance composition, as presented in this new Section.

Thanks are also due to Jane Scott-Barrett, choreographer of *Wild Child.* Her contributions, encouragement and support have helped to determine ways in which the work could be analysed and employed in a multimedia context, to further develop students' own creative dance composition work.

In addition, for their kind permission to use the photographs of *Wild Child,* I thank Deborah Barnard, Director of the Ludus Dance Company and Tara Martin, photographer. Thanks also go to the dancers featured in these photographs – Jason Bradley, Penny Collinson, Darryl Shepherd and Ruth Spencer. The other photographs, taken for the 3rd edition and retained in this 4th edition, were the work of Ryan Smith and feature Lisa Spackman, Christine Francis, Kevin Wright and Kate Oliver. Many thanks to these artists for the time and energy spent on this exercise.

INTRODUCTION

Dance Composition

DANCING AND COMPOSING DANCES

There is a vast difference between dancing and composing dances. Dancing can be enjoyed for the pleasure of moving with skilled accuracy, of moving with others and for the release of feeling. But to *compose a dance is to create a work of art*, and, according to Redfern (1973), an understanding of dance as an art form begins:

> . . . when concern is not simply with delight in bodily movement but with a formulated whole, a structured 'something' so that the relationship and coherence of the constituent parts becomes of increasing interest and importance. (p. 103)

Over the past three decades shifts in dance in education have been rapid and exciting and Redfern's recommendation for an emphasis on creating dances has been fulfilled. We have seen a move away from, or rather a refocusing of, the Laban model, which emphasised the experiential, child centred process of dancing as a means of developing personal qualities, towards a theatre art model with an emphasis on the dance product. However, the latter, in its professional form, proved too exacting for all but the few who could achieve the heights of technical perfection and polished performance. What we have now is what I like to call a 'midway' model – one that incorporates aspects of both the educational/process/Laban model and the professional/product/theatre model but also pays heed to the distinctive role that dance in education should have in a balanced curriculum.

Dance is a broad concept for there are many forms performed for varied reasons in many differing contexts. To experience a full diet of dance would take up much curriculum time so what we seem to have arrived at, as a consensus approach for dance in education in the new millennium, is a dance as art model which extends across, and draws from, a range of dance contexts – dance in the theatre, dance in the community and dance derived from specific cultural settings (e.g. South Asian classical dance, social dance, English folk dance).

DANCE AS ART

The 'midway' model amalgamates some elements of the 'educational' and 'professional' models yet introduces new aspects too. Its distinctiveness lies in the concept of *dance as art education* contributing towards *aesthetic education.* Concentration is centred upon pupils coming to know dance as art through composing, performing and appreciating dances. This three stranded approach has become the central organising principle of dance education today. There is a balance between creating, performing and viewing dances and an overall concern that pupils come to appreciate dances as art works, their own and those produced professionally in theatrical or performance settings.

The first edition of this book published in 1976 provided an important lead in developing and promoting this three stranded dance as art model for education. Since then, others have reiterated justifications for this conceptual basis for dance in education. The 1980s saw publications by Adshead (1981), Allcock and Bland (1980), Haynes in Abbs (1987), Lowden (1989) and the 1990s saw quite a proliferation of guidelines for dance in schools but mostly for the primary sector – viz. Harlow and Rolfe (1992), Evans and Powell (1994), Allen and Coley KS2 (1995), Davies and Sabin (1995), and Smith-Autard (1995). All these primary and the following secondary focused books (Harrison and Auty (1991), Allen and Coley KS3 (1995), and Killingbeck (1995)) reinforce the *Dance as Art* model. Added to this list, my second book, *The Art of Dance in Education* (1994), spells out in detail the conceptual bases and how the three processes of performing, composing and appreciating may be taught across the sectors – primary, secondary and higher education. Although, in this new edition of *Dance Composition*, some ideas on how the three strands may be integrated can be found in Section 3 (*Resource-based Teaching/Learning*), the main focus is obviously on the processes and practices of composing dances and, as such, the book is still an essential text for teachers and students.

THE NATURE OF COMPOSITION

Referring back to Redfern's statement above, composing involves the moulding together of compatible elements which, by their relationship and fusion, form an identifiable 'something'.

THE MATERIAL ELEMENTS

In order to effect this moulding successfully, the composer must be fully aware of the nature of the elements so that he/she may best judge how to select, refine and combine them. Think of the knowledge that necessarily goes into the making of an aircraft, a piece of furniture, a building. Maybe this knowledge is shared among many people, each concerned with a small part of the composition, but considered collectively, the nature of the elements are fully understood before such things can be produced. Without some previous concept or image it takes a great deal of trial and error to fashion anything with elements that are completely foreign.

METHODS OF CONSTRUCTION

The material elements of the composition need to be experienced and understood and, also, the processes or methods of fashioning or combining these various elements have to be learned and practised. The composer-musician cannot write notes *ad hoc*, they must have a relationship to each other in order to create melody. There are rules of construction which help the composer decide how to juxtapose sounds, achieve harmony or discord, change key, and vary phrase length and intensity, in order to produce mood or expression in the music. The composer also has to adhere to disciplines of rhythm, consider the effects of tempo and understand how to structure and stylise the piece. The dance composer has also to consider such matters. There are 'rules' or guidelines for construction which need to be part of the composer's awareness when making dances.

It is therefore clear that composition of a successful dance pre-supposes that the composer has knowledge of:

a) the material elements of a dance and
b) methods of construction which give form to a dance, together with
c) an understanding of the style within which the composer is working.

It is expected that a pupil who has only just been introduced to the art of making dances will not produce a work of art with the same degree of sophistication as a student who has undergone two or three years training.

Through experience and continual practice, the composer gradually acquires knowledge of movement material and methods of constructing with the material. The degree of this knowledge affects the resulting level of sophistication in the dance creations.

THE NATURE OF DANCE COMPOSITION – DANCE AS ART

From the discussion so far, it is clear that a dance composition should be regarded as a *work of art*. What, then, do we understand by the term *art*?

In her studio manual, *Materials of Dance*, Mettler (1960) writes:

> Art is the shaping of some material to provide aesthetic experience. (p. 399)

For the purposes of this book the term aesthetic will be used in the sense suggested by Reid (1969):

> We have an aesthetic situation wherever we apprehend and in some sense enjoy meaning immediately embodied in something; in some way unified and integrated; feeling, hearing, touching, imagining. When we apprehend – perceive, and imagine things and enjoy them for their own sakes – for their form – the forms seem to be meaningful to us, and this is an aesthetic situation. What we thus apprehend as meaningful is meaningful not in the sense that the perceived forms point to something else, their meaning, as ordinary words or other symbols do: the forms are in themselves delightful and significant – a poem, a picture, a dance, a shell on the sea shore. This then is the aesthetic, which art forms share with objects and movements which are not in themselves art at all. The arts are concerned with the aesthetic but the aesthetic is much wider than the arts. (pp.1–2)

This would suggest that expression of emotion is not necessarily art. To dance, release emotions and express oneself may well be an aesthetic experience, not only for the performer enjoying the movement for its own sake, but also for the onlooker. The sheer beauty of physical movement is aesthetically appreciated in many fields – athletics, sport, gymnastics, swimming, but this is not art.

A work of art is the expression or embodiment of something formed from diverse but compatible elements as a *whole entity* to be enjoyed aesthetically. It has to be created with the composer's intention to say something, *to communicate* an idea, or emotion. In dance this may be about people, happenings, moods or even about movement itself. The dance composition as an entity can only be a *portrayal* of emotions or ideas. Although sincerity of interpretation is essential in order to be convincing, the dancer does not actually 'feel' what the dance reflects. Rather, the carefully selected movement content is an abstraction from actual feeling or happenings to suggest meanings that are significant to the dance idea.

How the composition is arranged or shaped produces the *form* of the whole. The word *form** is used in all arts to describe the system through which each work of art exists. The idea or emotion which is to be communicated becomes embodied in the form. The form is the aspect which is aesthetically evaluated by the onlooker who does not see every element but gains an impression of the whole. This is particularly relevant to the temporal arts, such as music and dance.

This statement has been reinforced by Martin (1933) in the much used and still relevant quotation that follows.

> Form . . . may, indeed, be defined as the result of unifying diverse elements whereby they achieve collectively an aesthetic vitality which except by this association they would not possess. The whole thus becomes greater than the sum of its parts. The unifying process by which form is attained is known as composition.   (p.35)

TEACHING DANCE COMPOSITION

Teachers in art education, generally, are concerned that pupils eventually move from the experimental 'play' stage to a

*The following definition is appropriate for the word *form* as it is used in this book:

> The shape and structure of something as distinguished from its material of which it is composed.   Webster's Dictionary (1966)

construction stage in which they make things utilising the various components of the art form. As will be discussed later, pupils may well learn from ready-made dance compositions methods of combining elements to create whole dances. Even when the learner is attempting to replicate an art work emphasis of thought will be directed towards the 'rules' of construction.

In dance, too, we must go beyond the sheer 'activity of dancing' and devote time to the art of making dances. If the pupils are to experience dance as an art form, it is imperative that the dance teacher includes in the work-scheme a consideration of dance composition. Then, in addition to the experiential benefits of dancing, pupils may be guided into the realms of art and develop artistic talents and aesthetic awareness.

This view suggests that a reasonable assumption may be made on the following lines:

a) Knowledge of dance as an art form can only be acquired through experiencing dances, composing, performing and viewing them.

b) The basis for success in composition depends upon:
   1) the artistry and intuitive inspiration of the individual,
   2) a wide vocabulary of movement as a means of expression, and
   3) knowledge of how to create the shape and structure of a dance.

For the teacher of dance composition this assumption presents a difficulty. The trend of thought seems to indicate that, apart from knowledge of movement vocabulary and a cursory knowledge of form, dance composition merely requires intuitive artistic insight which is immeasurable and intangible. Although partly an inherited view from the Laban era, there are those who suggest that, because it is so subjective, it is not to be analysed and it is, therefore, unteachable. For this reason, perhaps, there is a dearth of literature on the subject. There are many books on the material content of dances but few offering ideas on how this content may be shaped and structured.

Hence, Section 1 offers a brief discussion of the dance composer's content. It pre-supposes that the reader already has, or will easily acquire from the text, a knowledge of the terminology and concepts offered by Rudolf Laban because, although the philosophy underlying his approach to dance in education is no longer valid, his analysis of movement elements as a basic tool for dance composition is unsurpassed. The concepts identified in his analysis are fundamental because Laban categorised the total range of human movement into easily recognisable and descriptive frames of reference.

Section 2, *Methods of Construction 1*, outlines the beginning processes in dance composition including improvisation, However, this is merely an introduction. A fuller discussion of improvisation was included in the 3rd edition, and remains here as an important discussion on a process that is germane in dance composition. This chapter – *Methods of Construction 7* – is placed later in the book as a reminder that experimentation through improvisation should take place throughout the process of composing a dance. It appears as a reminder, because the problem of how to achieve form in dance composition is the emphasised and central concern of the book and is discussed fully, as in previous editions, in the preceding chapters – *Methods of Construction 2–6.*

To this end the book focuses almost exclusively on traditional, formal approaches in dance composition because it is considered that artistic 'rules', established through generations of practice, need first to be learned and applied in many differing contexts before they can be broken, changed or ignored. These traditional principles of form are subjected to scrutiny in most of Section 2.

In the 3rd edition, Section 2 also contained an additional chapter, *Methods of Construction 8*, to identify *Alternative and Experimental Approaches* emerging from the work of recent practitioners. This was included, and is retained unaltered in this 4th edition, because such work challenges and will eventually change and replace the inherited mainstream approaches. It is considered important, therefore, that dance students study a range of new ideas and processes as an antithesis to established practice. Moreover, although much can be learned from viewing and reading about them, practical engagement with some of the alternative approaches is essential if the students are fully to understand, adopt and adapt such procedures for their own compositions. *Methods of Construction 8* provides a summary of some of the important characteristics of alternative approaches in professional dance contexts today, and indicates ways in which students might experiment to shift away from the more traditional, formal and established approaches.

Developments in the teaching of dance as an art form clearly demonstrate that the original content of this book outlined above remains relevant as a starting point for teachers and students of dance, whether undertaking professional training, teacher training, B.A. degree courses, G.C.S.E, 'A' level, BTEC or NVQ dance examination courses. It cannot be stressed enough, however, that this book is not in itself a prescribed course for the teaching of dance composition. (No one book can adequately provide all the ingredients necessary for the production of dance art works.) It does, however, disclose the important concepts and principles and offer some means of communicating them to learners. The pupils' imaginative employment of the concepts and principles presented here should be promoted through the teacher's carefully designed programme in which composing, performing and appreciating dances are experienced in a variety of contexts.

To this end, a good deal more material has been produced during the last decade. As well as using books such as this, teachers can enrich dance composing experiences for their pupils from resources such as live performances, videos and films of professional choreography, and/or practical workshops in choreography offered by dance artists resident in schools, colleges or local arts centres. The increasingly available notated scores provide a means of learning more about dance composition through reconstruction and performance of pre-choreographed excerpts from well-known dance works. In addition, there is a growth of agencies collecting resources, including videos, such as the National Resource Centre for Dance and The Place Dance Services in the UK, for example. All such resources are extremely valuable in teaching dance composition. Experience and knowledge gained from analysis and appreciation of professionally choreographed dance works, placed appropriately to supplement the teacher's own input, can effectively motivate, promote and boost pupils' progress in artistic learning.

An example of such a resource is presented in Section 3, *Resource-based Teaching/Learning in Dance Composition and New Technologies.* This 4th edition describes how the use of *Wild Child* – a CD resource pack published by Bedford Interactive Productions in conjunction with the Ludus Dance Company in 1999*

---

* See list of references at the back of the book for further details.

– can advance and greatly enhance students' composition work. This occurs by means of an in-depth study of a professional work to inform and inspire their own compositions. This 4th edition therefore takes cognisance of technology, not in its increasing integration in choreography as witnessed in the work of VTOL and Wayne McGregor, for example, but in ways in which it can be used to expose what is there in more mainstream choreography.

Clearly, as in all other arts, young composers need to learn about composition from the dance works of recognised choreographers. In dance, however, the bank of such resources is yet untapped for teaching and learning purposes. In my view, there are two main reasons for this. First, in comparison with other arts, there is still a very low number of resources available for such study in replayable recorded form, especially in contemporary dance. Second, analysis and discussion on paper with reference to performance in a live or linear video context remains at a fairly descriptive and general level, due to the difficulty of access and replay of details in the work.

There is little doubt that video resources of dance works have become essential in the teaching of dance appreciation. There are also increasing signs of an emerging pedagogy for the use of such resources in teaching/learning of composition. However, linear video that has not been especially shot for teaching/learning purposes, is not an entirely suitable format in that there is constant need to rewind and search for the required footage. Moreover, there are few videos with accompanying teaching materials that provide detailed study of choreographers' works, together with use of them as inspirational starting points for the students' own work.

Having now moved into the year 2000, as a profession we must surely advance in the use of technology for teaching/learning in dance. Resources recorded on digital video and delivered on CD or DVD formats seem to be the present direction to take. Detailed description of the *Wild Child* CD resource pack in Section 3 of this edition determines some of the ways in which technology can benefit teaching/learning of dance composition.

Section 4, *Standing Back from the Process* and Section 5, *Practical Assignments for Students* stand as they were in the 3rd edition. Rather than add further practical assignments, as indicated in the latter edition, there are many suggestions for practice in the chapters on *Improvisation* and *Alternative and Experimental Approaches in Dance Composition.* This is also the case in the new Section 3 of this edition – *Resource-based Teaching/Learning in Dance Composition and New Technologies.*

SECTION 1

The Material Content
Movement and Meaning

THE BASIC LANGUAGE OF MOVEMENT

The word 'language' is used here as an analogy only. It is not meant to suggest that the 'language' of movement can replace or be the same as language in a vocally communicative context. It is common knowledge that communication can take place through movement. How it communicates is the dance composer's area of study. Many verbal expressions describe moods or thoughts in movement terms:

'jumped for joy'	'shrank back in fear'
'rushed into the room'	'bent in pain'
'threw up his hands in horror'	'stamped in anger'
'didn't know which way to turn'	'shook with excitement'

It is this 'natural' movement language which forms the dance composer's vocabulary.

A child's movement is very expressive of his/her feelings. A mother seldom has to ask how he/she feels as she gets to know his/her symptomatic movement patterns. In our culture, it is expected that these are modified as we grow older so that, eventually, it is hard to tell what the typical British 'stiff upper lip' citizen might be feeling. In other cultures, restraint is not so marked, although it is generally accepted that one is not mature if one cannot withhold expression of emotions and moods. Often as much as we try to hide feelings, our involuntary movements and body stance give them away, regardless of what we may be saying vocally. The slumped body stance and slow heavy walk are easily seen to be symptomatic of depression or sadness, the tapping fingers of agitation or anger, the hands clenching and rubbing together of nervousness or fear.

ANALYSING THE LANGUAGE

The dance composer has this movement language as a basis but requires a means of analysing the content so that he/she may take the symptomatic human behaviour patterns, refine them, add to them, vary them, extract from them, enlarge them, exaggerate parts of them according to the needs in composition. The movement analysis which is most useful and comprehensive is that which Rudolf Laban presents in his books *Modern Educational Dance* and *Mastery of Movement*. Although one can refer to it as an analysis, in that it breaks down movement into various components, it does this only in a descriptive way. It is not a scientific breakdown such as is found in the sciences of anatomy, physiology, mechanics, biochemistry. It is a means by which anyone, with knowledge of Laban's principles, can *observe* and *describe* movement in detail.

It is not my intention to describe Laban's analysis in depth for the reader could find this in some of the books listed at the back of this book. Table 1 (opposite) is a simplified version which serves the immediate illustrative purposes.

CHOICE OF CONTENT

Laban's analysis of movement serves the dance composer well because it classifies movement into broad concepts, Each concept suggests a range of movement which may be explored. For example, let us take the concept of 'travel'. This is defined by Laban as a series of transferences of weight from one place to another. The intention is to move from A–B, and the word travel describes this, but it can be done in numerous ways. Each mode of travelling is characterised by the way in which the mover uses action, qualities of movement or dynamics (called effort in the translation of Laban's writings) and space, and how the dancer relates the travelling action to an object or person, if this is relevant. In dance, the choice of characterisation depends upon what the mover intends to convey. For instance, to express the joy of meeting the travel may take:

the action form of	leaps, hops, skips, turns, on the balls of the feet, with swinging arm gestures emphasising stretched limbs and body.
the qualities of	quick, accelerating, light, buoyant, free flowing or continuous.

TABLE 1

A summary of Laban's analysis of movement

Action of the body	Qualities of movement

Bend – Stretch – Twist
Transference of
  weight – stepping
Travel
Turn
Gesture
	Time – sudden – sustained
	              quick – slow
	
	Weight – firm – light
	                relaxed

Jump – five varieties
Stillness – balance
	Flow – free – bound
	            (on- (stop-
	            going) pable)

Body shapes
Symmetrical and
  asymmetrical use
Body parts – isolated –
  emphasised
	Combinations of two elements –
	  e.g. firm and sudden
	Combinations of three elements
	  e.g. light, sustained and free

Space environment	*Relationship*

Size of movement –
  size of space
Extension in space
Levels – low, medium
  and high
Shape in space –
  curved or straight
Pathways – floor patterns
  – air patterns
  curved or straight
Directions in space:
  the three dimensions
  planes
  diagonals
	Relating to objects –
	  relating to people
	Alone in a mass
	Duo: copying – mirroring
	          leading – following
	          unison – canon
	          meeting – parting
	          question and answer
	Group work: numerical
	                      variation
	                 group shape
	                 inter-group
	                 relationship
	                 Spatial relation-
	                      ships –
	                      over, under,
	                      around etc.

the spatial form of   forward in high level, large peripheral movements.

the relationship form of   moving towards another dancer.

On the other hand, to express dejection or distress, the travel may take:

the action form of   a slight run . . . into walk . . . into fall and slide on knees . . . body moving from stretched into curled shape . . . arms gesturing then falling to sides.

the qualities of   deceleration through the movement from quite quick to very slow, loss of tension from light tension to heavy relaxed feeling, the flow becoming more and more bound/held back.

the spatial form of   forward direction to low level moving on a straight pathway from centre to forward centre.

Thus the dance composer can use Laban's analysis to help the choice of movement content and depict the intention. He/she can choose the action and colour it with any qualitative, spatial or relationship content he/she likes so that the resulting movement expresses in the composer's own unique way what he/she intends it to say.

There is no *one* way of showing meaning in movement but there are accepted patterns, which define a general area of meaning, and which the composer should employ so that the work can be understood. These originate from the natural symptomatic movement language of humans. Invariably, people of different cultures will interpret what they see in different ways but, even so, there must be some consensus of opinion on such things as mood and idea which the work portrays. For example, if there were strong, striking, fighting, movements between two dancers, agreement will be on 'conflict' rather than 'harmony', or, if the movements were to be slow, gentle, surrounding, supporting, unified in time and complementary in space, it would show 'harmony' rather than 'conflict'.

LITERAL MOVEMENT INTO DANCE CONTENT

In addition to the major concern for choice of material that clearly identifies meaning, the dance composer has the responsibility of making movement content as original and interesting as possible. To do this Laban's analysis may be used as a frame of reference, and different combinations of action, qualities, space and relationship aspects can be tried. The idea of 'praying' will illustrate this point. Images in the mind of the literal human movement patterns connected with this concept kindles the imagination at the start – hands together, standing with head lowered, a fall on to the knees or even prostration. This range is made more extensive by the composer's analysis and subsequent handling of the movements. For instance, the hands together – head lowered movement can be taken:

action, qualitative and spatial form	While standing, from an open sideways extension of the arms, trace a peripheral pathway to forward medium, palms leading, slowly bringing the hands together, fingers closing last, with the head back. Then drawing the arms in towards the body centre, allow the chest to contract and curve inwards. To be taken with a sudden impulse at the beginning of the movement into a sustained closing of the hands – with increase of tension from fairly firm to very firm.
OR	Move the arms from a symmetric position in front of the head, elbows and wrists bent, successively right then left to diagonally high in front then down to the centre position. This should be done while walking in a forward direction four steps – head moving from low to high – with a firm slow quality throughout. The hands finish close but not touching.

It can be seen from these two examples that by having the basic symptomatic pattern in mind, the composer, through analysis, can identify what it embraces in terms of movement content, its action, its qualitative, its spatial usage and then utilise these aspects in his/her own way enlarging them, highlighting parts of the actions (e.g. the clasping hands), add actions (e.g. the trunk movement), alter the rhythm and dynamics or the spatial form.

In other words, the composer uses the analysis, first as a means of observing and identifying the nature of the movement as it is in everyday communication, and second, as a means of enriching it into dance content. This should ensure that the movement is both meaningful and interesting. It is difficult to retain a balance between meaning and originality. Care must be taken that the everyday movement origin has not been lost by too much enrichment. Nor should it be presented in the form of cliché which only leads to dull uninteresting work.

EXPLORING A RANGE OF MOVEMENT

The composer should, therefore, explore and experiment within a wide range, so that he/she becomes fully acquainted with movement and the feeling/meaning connotations. He/she should, at times, set out to explore a full range of movement without using it in composition, for this enriches movement experience and, inevitably, when starting to compose there is a better basis from which to make a choice of content. While exploring, the composer will consciously or intuitively experience the expressive properties of the movement, and the feel of it will be stored in the memory for future use. On the other hand, it may be that, while exploring movement for its own sake, an idea is evoked which will make a composition. In this way, movement itself becomes a stimulus for composition as the feeling has acted upon the composer, and then been transposed into content. To do this the composer must move from feeling to knowing – knowing what the movement is – analysing it and using its complexity as a starting point for the dance.

If, for instance, the dancer is engaged in exploration of turning as an action, he/she will be led by the teacher's or his/her own knowledge of the analysis, to take the action on both feet, on one foot, on one foot to the other, on different parts of the feet, with hops, jumps, steps, with leg and arm gestures leading into the action across the body or away from the body – producing inward or outward turns – spiralling from low to high and vice versa – taking a wide spread stepping turn – holding the leg high in the air whilst slowly pivoting on the supporting leg – initiating turns with various body parts and many more variations each having its own expressive content. The outward turns may have a feeling of exhilaration, while the hopping, jumping turns also express joy and excitement. An inward closed turn may suggest fear or turning away from something or someone. Turns which increase in speed generate excitement. A slow wandering turn may suggest searching. While the dancer is actually performing the movement, he/she should have some kind of feeling about it. Even if he/she cannot name a mood or emotion that is evoked when it merely feels 'nice', 'good', or 'clever', it carries with it a 'colour' and mode of being. All movements have expressive properties which are employed as a means of communicating ideas about human feelings, events or even about the movements themselves.

MOVEMENT AND MEANING

It should be clear that movement is a vast communicating language and that varieties of combinations of its elements constitute many thousands of movement 'words'. Also, in the context of a dance, movements have to be understood as meaningful in juxtaposition with others. Very often it is a phrase of actions that portrays a single 'word' meaning, or conversely, one movement can give a whole 'paragraph' of content. To transform a vocabulary of movement into meaningful visual images, the composer is dealing with three intangible elements: movement, time and space. How the meaning can be enhanced by the composer's use of time and space will be discussed later. Meaning in the movement itself is of importance now.

Presentation of literal movement is not dance. The art of mime aims for realistic representation of movement to communicate literal meaning. Dance often uses conventional and mime-based gestures but the composer may choose to manifest the idea in a more symbolic way. This is done by abstracting an essence from the literal movement which is then given a unique flavour through artistic manipulation. Similarly the poet may, rather than make direct statements, use metaphor and simile to establish images which can have several possible meanings within the poem's context.

Although it derives from fundamental human movement, symbolic dance movement imagery can pose several interpretative possibilities. To a certain extent, it depends upon the nature of the audience as to how 'open to interpretation' the composer can make the dance. Some audiences, wishing to be entertained without much effort, require readily recognised movement images, while others tend to enjoy looking more deeply.

The following description of a particular dance may help to explain a little about the range of movement imagery open to a composer, and the scope of interpretation some particular movement images present to an audience.

Solo dance titled 'Confession' ...
Music – single instrument – slow, smooth, introspective, quiet and harmonic.

1) Movements included:
   a) closing and crossing movements of arms and legs,
   b) peripheral arm gestures to cover head,
   c) opening and extending arms and legs very low to the ground,
   d) stepping and opening sideways, arms high and to side, wrists flexed palms up, chest high and the head up,
   e) closing one hand above the other and both hands above head but not touching,
   f) hands clasped with fully stretched arms in varying directions,
   g) hands opening and extending with wrists and forearms touching
   h) twisting trunk movement with palms of hands near the face,
   i) forward and backward rocking movements with leg gestures extending just off the ground, arms held close to the body,
   j) falling to the knees into sideways roll returning to one knee and extending forward,
   k) turning from open body positions into closed body positions,
   l) jumps with arms and one leg high in front,
   m) travelling with long low runs and ending suddenly in a fall.

These are a few examples of the movements in the dance. The description is hardly full enough for the reader to be able to translate it into movement but a range of movement ideas should be apparent and something of the composer's interpretation of the dance idea may have emerged.

2) Interpretations:
   a) something to do with religious confession – the confessing person feels shame, prays, shows humility, reverence and confidence in receiving forgiveness;
   b) something to do with confessing a feeling of love – the confessing person feels guilty and afraid yet joyful in the revelation of a hitherto hidden feeling of love;
   c) something to do with a penitent criminal feeling remorse, shame, self-pity and a dawning of hope in anticipation of freedom.

The composer might have had one of these ideas in mind. The first few movements would suggest an interpretation of the title to each viewer and each would then 'read' the images to fit into the interpretation. If a dance is as 'open' as this, the composer has extended the movement content away from the literal and into the realms of symbolism. The symbols themselves are recognisable in this dance for all the interpretations acknowledge 'confession' but the contexts of the confessions vary. The symbols therefore act as suggestions and finer details in interpretation are left to the viewer's imagination.

STYLISING THE MATERIAL CONTENT

The above text has considered a range of natural movements as a source for dance expression. However, there are a number of pre-formulated, tried and tested dance techniques which also constitute an essential part of the dance composer's repertoire. For further discussion on various techniques, the concept of style and processes of stylising dance material, readers should proceed to *Methods of Construction 6.*

SECTION 2

Methods of Construction 1
The Beginnings

STIMULI FOR DANCE

A stimulus can be defined as something that rouses the mind, or spirits, or incites activity.

Stimuli for dance compositions can be auditory, visual, ideational, tactile or kinesthetic.

AUDITORY STIMULI

Auditory stimuli include music, the most usual accompaniment for dances. Very often, the dance composer starts with a desire to use a certain piece of music, the nature of which has stimulated a dance idea. There are many kinds of music, and the dance composer must be aware of the nature of the music (emotive, atmospheric, abstract, lyrical, comic, dramatic, architecturally patterned) so that if it is to be used as the accompaniment, it complements rather than conflicts with the idea.

The music not only dictates the kind of dance, but also its mood, its style, its length, phrasing, intensities and overall form. Music, therefore, provides a structured framework for the dance, and the stimulus becomes more than a springboard beginning. If music is used as accompaniment, the dance cannot exist without it.

Sometimes, a dance composer may be inspired by a piece of music and, because of its complexity or purity, decide not to use it as accompaniment. In this case, perhaps the quality, or design, in the music could be taken and transposed into dance content. The dance form that emerges need not emulate the form of the piece of music and, when it is complete, the dance should be able to exist for itself without reference to the stimulus.

Other auditory stimuli include percussion instrument sounds, human voice sounds, words, songs and poems. The mood, character, rhythm and atmosphere of the dance can exist without the sound accompaniment. For instance, a poem may have been the stimulus, but the dance composer finds he/she cannot interpret all the words into movement, so uses it in a different way. Maybe, it is decided necessary to hear the poem before viewing the dance, or to hear a few lines, which make the essence of it, as punctuation of the movement giving its meaning. On the other hand, once it has stimulated the idea or mood, the dance composer may not need to use the poem at all. The composer may even turn to another source for accompaniment, music perhaps. If, however, the poem is used as accompaniment for the dance, the two must appear to the viewer as inseparable in the manifestation of the idea,

Percussion instrument sounds, human voice sounds, sounds in nature or the environment, often make interesting and dynamic stimuli for dance. Here, the movement interpretation can be purely imitative in quality and duration, or perhaps, the association of ideas related to the sounds could provoke emotional, comic, or dramatic interpretations. There is far less restriction than is the case with music in the way that these stimuli can be used, and the dance composer has to take care that the dance and the sound accompaniment have form which give structural unity.

VISUAL STIMULI

Visual stimuli can take the form of pictures, sculptures, objects, patterns, shapes, etc. From the visual image, the composer takes the idea behind it, as he/she sees it, or its lines, shape, rhythm, texture, colour, utilitarian purpose, or other imagined associations. A chair, for instance, may be viewed for its lines, its angularity, its purpose in holding the body weight, or it may be seen as a throne, a trap, an object to hide behind or under, an instrument for defending oneself, or as a weapon.

Visual stimuli provide more freedom for the dance composer in that, often, the dance stands alone and unaccompanied by the stimulus. However, the dance should make the origin clear if it is to be an interpretation of it.

KINESTHETIC STIMULI

It is possible to make a dance about movement itself. Some movement or movement phrase takes on the role of kinesthetic stimulus, and the dance is derived from this basis. The movement, in this case, has no communicative purpose other than the nature of itself. It does not intend to transmit any given idea but it does have a style, mood, dynamic range, pattern or form, and these aspects of the movement, or movement phrase, can be used and developed to form the dance which is an exposition on movement itself.

TACTILE STIMULI

Tactile stimuli often produce kinesthetic response which then becomes the motivation for dances. For example, the smooth feel of a piece of velvet may suggest smoothness as a movement quality which the composer uses as a basis for the dance. Or, the feel and movement of a full skirt may provoke swirling, turning, freely flowing, spreading movements which then become the main impetus for the dance composer.

A tactile stimulus could also become an accompanying object. A very fine piece of material, for instance, could be manipulated by the dancers and form a moving part of the dance, complementing, linking, dividing, enveloping and following the dancers. It is important, however, that the manipulation of the stimulus does not become the overriding part of the dance, the dancers' movement appearing secondary.

IDEATIONAL STIMULI

Ideational stimuli are perhaps the most popular for dances. Here the movement is stimulated and formed with intention to convey an idea or unfold a story. If the idea to be communicated is war, immediately the composer's range of choice is limited to movement that will suggest this. Ideas, therefore, have a certain aura of concepts which provide frameworks for the creation of dances. Furthermore, stories or happenings have to be sequentially portrayed in narrative form.

TO CONCLUDE

The stimulus forms the basic impulse behind the work and then goes on to structure it. Some structure the outcome more forcefully than others. Often, several stimuli collectively will influence the work and perhaps, as in the case of music, the stimulus accompanies the dance.

The dance composer's concern is, firstly, whether or not the stimulus is suitable and how to look at it, and, secondly, how it is to accompany the dance if this is to be the case. This concern may derive from a wish that the dance portray enough of the stimulus to be clear in intention. Obscurity of purpose will cause it to fail in communication. The stimulus is the basis of the motivation behind the dance. If the composer has deliberately created an interpretation of the inspiration incited by the stimulus, and he/she intends that the dance be understood as such, the stimulus should clearly stand out as an origin, even if it is not present.

This suggests that the dance composer has to decide whether or not successful communication of the idea *depends* upon knowledge of the stimulus as an origin. Perhaps it is not necessary for the audience to know the original stimulus, since the dance outcome, as in the case of a dance inspired by a piece of music which has not been used as accompaniment, may well be able to stand on its own, without reference to the stimulus. Often though, the dance title suggests the original stimulus, enough at least to comprehend the motivation. In any event, whether apparent in the outcome or not, the stimulus dictates the type of dance.

Broad classification of dances is generally quite simple for, like music or any other art, we accept terms such as Classical, Modern, Ethnic, Jazz, Pop.

Commonly accepted terms are also used when describing types of dance composition more specifically. These include pure, study, abstract, lyrical, dramatic, comic and dance-drama.

A PURE DANCE AND A STUDY

We say pure dance when we mean that it has originated from a kinesthetic stimulus and deals exclusively with movement itself.

A study is pure, but a dance can be pure and be more than a study. A study suggests that the composer has concentrated on a limited range of material. For example, a picture may be called a study when it is portraying a bowl of fruit, or a portrait may fit the description. In music, a study is often in one key and perhaps within a certain range of technical skills. The dance study may be confined to one kind of movement, perhaps rise and fall or a scale range of time. A dance which is described as pure, generally has no limitations of movement range. In fact it may have several sections in it, each of which has different movement emphasis.

The movement content in a pure dance may be simpler for the performer than that in a study. The latter often demands more complex movement and aims to show virtuosity and academic understanding of its chosen content.

The ballet *Etudes* choreographed by Harald Lander provides an example. The total ballet may be classified as a pure dance, yet each small part in isolation can be described as a study. To mention two, there is a study on the *plié* section of the barre work, and a study on *petite batterie*, but collectively, the whole ballet gives an overall view of the phases and total rhythm of the ballet class. Because the idea is about a certain style of movement, the ballet is pure in classification. Further examples of pure ballets include George Balanchine's *Symphony in C* and *Agon*, and Frederick Ashton's *Symphonic Variations*, where the movement itself as interpretation of the music becomes the basis for beautifully formed works of art.

ABSTRACT DANCE

Abstract is a confusing term. In the fine art sense, Webster's Dictionary (1966) offers the following definition:

> . . . presenting or possessing schematic or generalised form, frequently suggested by having obscure resemblance to natural appearances through contrived ordering of pictorial or sculptural elements.

Of dance composition, however, the dictionary defines *abstract* as:

> . . . lacking in concrete program or story.

This latter definition is wide and meaningless. If a dance lacks a story it is not necessarily abstract. If it lacks concrete programme it can have no logical development, clear manifestation or communication. In which case it is not a dance. Often, young dance composers think they are 'with it' and very modern if they present a series of unrelated and therefore 'non-programme' movements as an abstract dance. Perhaps it works in the static visual arts for the viewer has time to ponder, look from all angles, and read meaning into it as he/she wishes. The dance audience cannot look and ponder. A temporal art cannot be abstract in this sense of the work, its images must somehow be linked and connected.

If we accept the definition pertaining to fine art, then we see that the dance composer could justifiably portray images which are *abstracted* from the natural and bear resemblance to it. Obscurity, however, should be avoided. There is no time to delve into depths in order to find hidden resemblances to the natural, these should appear easily and very quickly. Maybe several *abstractions* can be put over in the manifestation of one idea, e.g. 'shape'. The dance is abstract when it is the *result of abstraction*, which is:

> ... something that comprises or concentrates in itself the essential qualities of a larger thing or several things.
> Webster's Dictionary (1966)

Like the 'shape' dance, a dance entitled 'magnetism', or a dance entitled 'time', which portrays a variety of images based upon the phenomenal and human aspects of the concept, could be examples of concentration on 'a larger thing', whereas a dance entitled 'conformity', which portrays images of following in step pattern, imitating mannerisms, waiting one's turn in a queue, might be an example of concentration upon the essential quality of 'conformity' in several otherwise unrelated things.

Thus an abstract dance implies that the composer has abstracted some thought about one thing or several things, and identifies these through movement images which bear fairly close resemblance to them.

LYRICAL DANCE

Lyrical dance is a category often used and is quoted in Webster's Dictionary (1966) as:

> ... a tender dance   *Dance Observer*

In reference to the song as a lyric composition, the dictionary defines it as:

> ... having a relatively light, pure, melodic quality

It is unnecessary to categorise this as a separate type, for it suggests poetic mood which may well be a dominant characteristic of a pure dance or even an abstract dance. The term 'lyrical', therefore, suggests the quality of a dance.

DRAMATIC DANCE AND DANCE-DRAMA

Dramatic dance implies that the idea to be communicated is powerful and exciting, dynamic and tense, and probably involves conflict between people or within the individual. The dramatic dance will concentrate upon a happening or mood which does not unfold a story. Dance-drama, on the other hand, has a story to tell and does so by means of several dramatic dance episodes or scenes sequentially arranged. A dance depicting Lady Macbeth's agony of mind would be a dramatic dance, but portrayal of the actual story of Macbeth would be dance-drama.

Because dramatic dance and dance-drama are concerned with emotions and happenings related to people, characterisation is a prominent feature. The composer has carefully to study character and mood in reality, and understand how to dramatise the movement content for dance. This, he/she learns, is done through exaggeration of the action, qualitative or space characteristics, particular development of the rhythmic patterns and emphasis on body shape and stance.

Stress on the qualitative content in movement always tends to give dramatic impact. Also, in a dramatic dance there is nearly always relationship between people, or between an individual and an object, and these relationships are always emotive. However, orientation of the relationship must not remain strictly between dancers and the confines of their space. The composer should take care that the audience also can identify with the dramatic relationships within the dance. Projection of dramatic involvement is a difficult technique in dance composition. The composer must try many ways of putting this across. Perhaps spatial placement, directional alignment and the use of focus are of paramount importance.

COMIC DANCE

Another category, which must be included, is comic dance. Movement material requires a certain kind of handling if it is to be comic. Essentially original or unusual ways of moving and relating to the environment and other people can be comic. Comic movement might be achieved by making body parts move in peculiarly co-ordinated ways taking them out of their normal space zones. Inverting the stance, performing movements which are usually taken on the vertical plane on a horizontal plane, stressing the use of the face and very small body parts like the fingers or toes, could make comic movement. Perhaps also, the composer should try for the unpredictable in movement. For instance, a very large, grand, sweeping gesture with travel on a circular pathway finished with stillness and just one finger moving up and down!

Very often comic dances are mimetic in nature or have parts which are mimetic. The movement content here can be very representational of real life or, perhaps, have deviations or exaggerations of certain elements which cause comedy.

MODE OF PRESENTATION

It is necessary to discuss *how* the movement content is to be presented by the dance composer.

Supposing a decision has been made on the type of dance to be composed and the accompaniment, if there is any. It is quite probable that the stimulus which prompted the idea brought into the composer's thought images of movement related to his/her own experience, which convey the idea, feeling, mood or happening. For example, 'sadness' conjures up images of people bent, slow moving, introvert small movements, swaying, hand wringing, head in hands, etc. In a dance to depict these human movements exactly as they are in real life, is to utilise the movement in a purely *representational* way. To use these movements, extracting the essence or main characteristics and adding other features in action or dynamic stresses, is to utilise the movement in a *symbolic* way.

To symbolise something suggests that there must be a certain sign or signal which details its origin, and the other aspects of it may be unique and perhaps unreal. For example, a gentle sway in sadness may be taken as a large body movement into side extension followed by a circular upper trunk movement with a turn.

Pure representational presentation is mime and from this extreme there are degrees of representation through symbols to the most 'symbolic' and least representative which is a *nearly* unrecognisable presentation. The word 'nearly' is stressed because if it *is* unrecognisable then it fails. The least representative to reality makes the movement 'open ended' in that there may be quite a number of interpretations as to its meaning. This may be because the signal that the composer chooses to retain is very weak juxtaposed to his/her own unique embellishments. Nevertheless, something within the range of possible representative meaning must be clear to the onlooker.

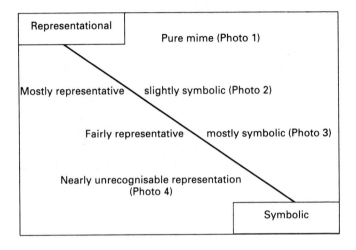

The composer, then, stimulated by his/her own experience of meaning in movement, decides how to present the meaning, representing it as it is in real life, or symbolically portraying it in an original way. Most dances are symbolic presentations of movement, but if they are to be successful the symbols must be identifiable and meaningful to the audience.

IMPROVISATION

The composer has already made some decisions before beginning to move. A decision to use a certain stimulus or several stimuli has inspired thoughts about the kind of dance to be composed, i.e., comic, abstract, dramatic. In deciding this, the composer has also foreseen the kind of presentation he/she is to use, i.e. symbolic – representational.

1

2

3

4

Now is the moment to start composing. He/she experiments with movement and tries to realise imagined movement images into real movement expression. This initial exploration is called *improvisation.*

Improvisation which comes purely from within, a sheer abandonment in movement to indulge the feeling, is not often the kind of improvisation used by the dance composer. As suggested by H'Doubler (see the quotation in the Introduction) this feeling may well be tapped and recaptured by the composer.

When dancers are moving to a piece of music, the improvisation which emerges is less free because the mood and 'colour' of the music suggest the interpretation, and indicate moving in a certain way – governed by the changes in tempo, tone, pitch, etc., and its style, form and character. The experimentation with movement is confined to that which is suitable *interpretation* of the music, and this kind of improvisation – although more limited – is commonly used as a starting point.

The Beginnings of Composition

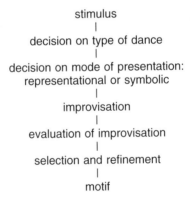

stimulus
|
decision on type of dance
|
decision on mode of presentation:
representational or symbolic
|
improvisation
|
evaluation of improvisation
|
selection and refinement
|
motif

Improvisation is spontaneous, transient creation – it is not fixed, it is not formed. During improvisation, there are moments when a movement 'feels right' and fits the composer's image. When this occurs, the improvised movement phrase can be recaptured to provide the basic ingredients for the composition. The movement or movement phrase which evolves in this way may be a suitable starting point for the composition process. In evaluating this matter, the composer may use one or more of the following criteria:

1) that the movement has meaning and relevance to the idea for the dance;
2) the movement is interesting and original in action, dynamics and spatial patterning;
3) the movement has potential for development.

This evaluation pre-supposes considerable knowledge of both material and form, a knowledge which is acquired through experience. The apprentice-composer starts from *feeling*, not knowing, and may select a movement starting point intuitively. Success is limited, however, if intuition only is relied upon for too long. The reverse can, also, present problems, as knowing without feeling often produces sterile, uninteresting and purely academic dances. Feeling and knowing should always be interrelated. How feeling can consciously be brought into knowing and remain as an artistic stimulus will be discussed later.

The movement starting point is the first piece of composition. It has been selected, evaluated and refined, and is now set as the initial motivating force for the rest of the dance. This movement or movement phrase is called the *motif.*

The composer continues to employ improvisation in developing, varying and elaborating on the starting motif, and finding new ones for the rest of the composition.

Methods of Construction 2
Motif into Composition

TO RECAP

Creativity is a quest for order. When we create we aim for completeness and logical design. Every part of the whole should seem necessary and inevitable.

For the dance to be a meaningful whole it must have recognisable form. A whole is made from a number of components and the dance composer's components include:

1) each dancer's body as an instrument which has volume, shape and action capacities;
2) movement which has physical properties of time, weight, and flow – the interaction of which determines the form and style of the action;
3) the space environment which can be shaped by movement;
4) the relationships that the body can make with other things or people.

ARRANGEMENT OF MATERIAL

How the components are arranged produces the form of the work of art:

> Art expression, like form created by a shifting kaleidoscope, is forever changing, forever new. The myriad of geometric designs that one sees in the kaleidoscope are all made from the same elements, variously shaped pieces of coloured glass but as the relationships of these coloured objects to each other are changed, new forms ensue.
>
> Hayes (1955), p. 1

In dances, too, the elements of the composer's movement vocabulary are arranged so that they have various relationships to each other. Yet if the dance is successful, the patterning or juxtapositioning of movements is *not* the noticeable feature. A gymnastic sequence or skating programme would more favourably fit the analogy with a kaleidoscope, for it is the skilful arrangement of known movement skills that makes successful and aesthetic results in these activities.

FORM

A dance aims to communicate an idea and, therefore, there is much more to it than the mere arranging of movements. It has a *form*, an overall shape, system, unity, mould or mode of being. This outer shell, or constructional frame, is the outstanding feature which supports the inner arrangement of its components. Having seen a dance, the viewer does not remember each and every movement or their order. Rather, he/she remembers the impression of the whole, its shape, whether it rounded off as it began, the excitement of the development into the climaxes, the main message it conveyed and how original and interesting was the overall impact.

So the composer has two main tasks. Simultaneously and with artistic awareness he/she should:

1) select movement content, utilising the dancer/s;
2) set the movement into a constructional frame which will give the whole its form.

– The Motif Development and Variation –

THE MOTIF

There must be *a foundation* for logical development or form. The foundation of a dance is its initial motif. This has emerged during improvisation through the influence of the stimulus, the composer's artistic imagination, and his/her movement interpretation of the two.

Webster's Dictionary (1966) defines the word *motif* as:

> . . . a theme or subject – an element in a composition especially a dominant element.

Langer (1953) says (author's italics):

> The fundamental forms which occur in the decorative arts of all ages and races – for instance the circle, the triangle, the spiral, the parallel – are known as motifs of design. They are not art 'works', not even ornaments, themselves, but they lend themselves to . . . artistic creation. The word motif bespeaks this function: *motifs are organising devices that give the artist's imagination a start, and so 'motivate' the work. They drive it forward and guide its progress.*
>
> Some of these basic shapes suggest forms of familiar things. A circle with a marked centre and a design emanating from the centre suggest a flower, and that hint is apt to guide the artist's composition. All at once a new effect springs into being, there is a new creation – a representation, the illusion of an object . . . The motif . . . and the feeling the artist has toward it, give the first elements of form to the work: its dimensions and intensity, its scope, and mood. (p. 69)

Preston-Dunlop (1963) states:

> A movement motif is a simple movement pattern but it has in it something capable of being developed. (p. 184)

The beginning motif starts to communicate the idea and the next few phrases need to go on saying the same thing as further qualification of the statement. Because dance is transient this restatement is very important. The musician may establish a melody in the opening bars, and then continue repeating the tune, developing it and varying it but keeping its characteristics until it has been well established – then, maybe, another melody is introduced which intersperses with the first. The dance composer has also to establish a movement phrase, develop and vary it, so that is becomes known to the viewer, before the dance goes on to say more about the subject.

How is this done? The motif can be as long as a 'verse' or as short as a 'word'. If it is the latter, then, maybe it is necessary to repeat it exactly at the beginning so that it is established clearly. *Repetition of the content, however, is mostly achieved by means of development and variation of the motif/s.*

A MOTIF

Let us assume that the motif is the simple action of side step and close. This action is taken using the feet for transference of weight, right foot starting. It is danced using a degree of time and force – is hesitant or continuous in flow, moves in a side-ways right direction in relation to the body front, which is facing front in relation to the stage space. The rest of the body remains in the normal standing position.

DEVELOPMENT AND VARIATION – USING ACTION FEATURES

The motif could be repeated again exactly, using the left foot to begin. It could be taken using a different part of the foot to take weight, for instance, on the balls of both feet – on the heels of both – on the ball of the right foot and heel of the left – on the inside edges of the feet – with the weight passing through the balls to the whole foot. There are many ways. It may be that the initiating foot could lead into the side step with the sole of the foot – or side – or ball – or heel – or edge – or top surface. Or, it may be that the closing foot could be used in such a manner, emphasising a leading part, or taking weight in a particular and different way. The action could emphasise the property of stretch, or bend, or twist in the legs, or accompanying body parts. Arm gesture could be added with one or both arms. Leg gesture could be emphasised into the side step, or on the closure, or both. The side and close could be repeated a number of times into a direction of travel, and it could be taken with a turn or change of body front. It could have elevation added to it, into the side step, or the close, or both. It could be taken with a transference of weight onto the knees. Possibly just the side step could be emphasised leaving out the close, or vice versa. The close step, for instance, could be taken by the right foot in contact with the left leg into standing – or crossing over in front of, or behind, the left leg, thereby concentrating on one aspect of the action, extracting it from the rest. The action could be taken with symmetric use of the body, both feet sliding sideways and closing simultaneously with the body evenly placed around its centre. One side of the body could be considerably more emphasised than the other on the side step and perhaps answered by the other side being emphasised on the closing step, giving the whole an asymmetric flavour. Further variation could be achieved by altering the body flow – body parts moving in succession or simultaneously.

DEVELOPMENT AND VARIATION – USING QUALITATIVE FEATURES
The qualities or dynamic content of the motif could be developed and varied at the same time as, or apart from, the above action developments. The motif could be repeated faster or slower, with acceleration and deceleration – one part of it could be sudden and the other sustained. Thus the time rhythm of the motif could be varied. The energy stress could be increased or decreased – from strong to gentle qualities. The side step may be taken as a stamp and the close with very little tension or vice versa. Different time and weight combinations could be utilised to give rhythmic patterning. The flow in the motif could be interrupted and held back to give a hesitant quality, or it could be continuous and ongoing in nature – particularly if a series of side and close steps were taken driving into one direction.

DEVELOPMENT AND VARIATION – USING SPATIAL FEATURES

The composer's use of the space environment could be presented as another means of development. The side and close step could be small, or large, thus defining how much space it takes. It could be taken at different levels, low, medium, or high, and in different directions. This latter would be effected by maintaining the sideways direction of the side step in relation to the body front but changing the direction of the body front in relation to the space environment. Whilst this is done, the action of turning must be employed, and a floor pattern will emerge. The shape or pathway that the movement creates in the air may be emphasised as a development feature – for instance, the right leg could gesture into the sideways step with an arc-like action, accompanied by the arms taking a large outward circling movement, and the closing action could be accompanied by an inward circling of the legs and arms, using less space by bending the knees and elbows. The pathways that emerge could be repeated in different directions, thus making a spatial pattern.

DEVELOPMENT AND VARIATION – USING THE RELATIONSHIP FEATURES

The relationship of the parts of the motif to each other could be altered: the closing step done first, then the side step, thus reversing the order. This is more easily illustrated by taking a longer motif like – travel – jump – turn – still. It could be done in reverse order or in different orders. Parts of it could be extracted, used and put back into the original juxtaposition.

REPETITION AS A CONSTRUCTIONAL ELEMENT

The word repetition means *exactly the same thing again.* In the art sense, and in my opinion, the word has wider connotations which could be illustrated as shown opposite.

Therefore, the notion of repetition as a constructional element implies that the material is manipulated to:

1) restate or say again exactly – the mover might do identically the same which could be performed with the other side of the body;

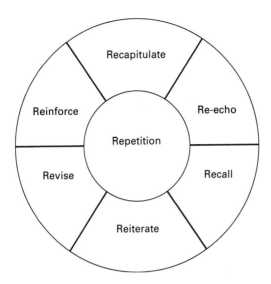

2) reinforce – making part or the whole of the movement motif more emphasised; this could be done by making the movements larger, or adding more tension, or defining the movements by moments of stillness;

3) re-echo suggests that something of the material which has passed returns into the new content;

4) recapitulate means that the statements occur again shortening or telescoping the content;

5) revise – to go over again in some detail, making some parts even clearer;

6) recall means to bring back into the memory; in the new material the onlooker is reminded of something that has gone before; the content can be dissimilar, but there is an apparent association;

7) reiterate – stresses the fact of repetition; there may be several continuous repetitions which perhaps die away.

While the composer is using repetition in the expanded sense, A range of developments and variations of the motifs (Table 2, overleaf) will inevitably emerge. This should ensure that the content is interesting and yet recognisable as *repeated* material.

TABLE 2

ACTION

1. Same again – or on other side
2. Use of different body parts
3. Addition of actions – bend, stretch, twist, travel, turn, gesture, stillness, jump, stepping
4. Variation of body flown simultaneous and successive
5. Subtraction of action from motif
6. Symmetric or asymmetric emphasis

QUALITY

1. Same again
2. Speed change
3. Weight variation
4. Time-weight variation
5. Flow variation
6. Contrasting qualities

REPETITION through development and variation by:

SPACE

1. Use of same space pattern
2. Variation of space pattern:
   size
   levels
   extension – near – far
   directions
   pathways – on floor
     in the air
3. Body shape, line in space

RELATIONSHIP

Variation of relationship through changing the juxtapostion of move- ments within motifs

TYPES OF MOTIF

It is impossible to enumerate the types of motifs that every dance composer is likely to use. Each dance has its own motifs, and each motif has its own characteristics shared by no other.

It is possible, however, to generalise to a certain extent in description of motifs in terms of length and content emphasis.

LENGTH OF MOTIFS

Some dances use 'positional 'motifs. These positions are moved 'into' and 'out of', and act as the landmarks or foundations around which the rest of the dance movement is formed. The motifs, in this instance, are in existence for a short time as momentary positions.

On the other hand, a motif may last for a length of time and could consist of seven or eight movements which create one, two, or even three, movement phrases. It may be that this length of statement is necessary to say one or several things in the dance. It could be presented as a whole, which often happens when the dance is an interpretation of a song or poem. Words in songs or poems are mostly arranged into verse lengths, and the movement can echo this. It is easy for the audience to remember the content because the words in the song or poem become signals for certain parts of the motifs. Very long motifs presented in their entirety without such helpful accompaniment, tend to make it difficult for the onlooker to follow.

Long motifs could be built up piece by piece such as:

```
      movement 1
           "      1    then 2
           "      1     "  2     then 3
           "      1     "  2      "  3      then 4 etc
or movement  1    then development of 1
           "      2      "        "        "  2
           " 1 and 2 development and variation of both
           " 3 development of 3
           " 1, 2 and 3 development and variation into 4
```

In the final outcome it is only the composer and the dancers who know exactly the length and structure of the motifs which have been used as constructional elements, foundational to the rest of the dance. They need not necessarily be apparent to the onlooker. Unless there is definite association with the stimulus in defining the duration of each motif, their length should be indistinguishable.

CONTENT EMPHASIS

The nature of the motif may be descriptive in terms of the emphasis it has in content. It is possible to note action, quality or space stresses and follow these aspects as the motivational forces behind the outcome of the dance.

A dance may be space stressed. For instance, the curved shapes and pathways the dancer makes in the space may be the motifs which the audience would view, rather than the action/quality content. In this case the dancer emphasises the shaping of space through projection into the environment and, if this is successful, the audience will follow these patterns. As a basis for the rest of the dance, the patterns in space then become developed, varied and contrasted into a completed dance form.

The quality content of movement may become the distinguishing feature of the motif. The composer may choose to retain a slow, light and flowing movement quality to establish a quiet feeling and while doing this will use a number of actions. On repeating the quality or developing it, the composer must also concentrate on retaining an identity within the action content. There can be no quality without action. The two cannot really be dissociated, but the slowness, lightness and flowing qualities could be more emphasised than the steps, travels, turns and gestures through which the qualities emerge. The dancer's intention has a great influence on how the audience views the dance. If the dancer concentrates on communication of the quality within the motif, the action content should almost become secondary to it.

An action-based motif is perhaps the easiest to handle. Action motifs can be broken down and put together again, since each piece is identifiable as a separate entity, e.g. turn, travel, fall, roll, rise, jump. Actions themselves have inherent meanings and emphasis on the action content can make the quality and space aspects less apparent. Nevertheless, the manner in which each action is performed in terms of quality and its spatial usage is all part of its identity.

Movement is an interrelation of action, quality and space and no one aspect can exist without the others in the motifs, but one or two can be more emphasised. The dance composer could aim for equal emphasis on all three aspects of the movement content in a motif, and make the movement relate to an object or person. The first motif establishes the movement emphasis for that part of the dance. It might be rich in content and become clarified and simplified as the dance progresses or conversely, very simple to start with and become richer and more elaborate during the composition.

For most dances the total range of movement content is available to the composer.

– *The Dance Design in Time* –

THE LENGTH OF TIME A MOVEMENT TAKES
The composer must be concerned that the dance, which exists through time, uses time in a constructive and interesting way. Movement takes time and it is easy to understand that this time can vary in length or duration. The successful composer, therefore, considers the quick, moderate and slow aspects of movement and tries to use them in forming interesting time patterns which are relevant to the idea.

THE LENGTH OF THE DANCE
The time aspect is part of the total rhythm of the dance. This is discussed in more detail in *Methods of Construction 4.* It is enough to mention here that the dance composer should be aware of the total *length* of the dance as vital to the communication of the idea. Dances that are too long lose their impact, and dances that are too short either leave the onlooker surprised and wishing for more, or puzzled – not having had enough to understand the meaning.

The composer should also be aware of the total time picture in relation to the beginning, middle and end of the dance. The beginning may be long, unfolding its content with care, or it may have a vital impact which 'simmers down'. The end may die away gradually into finality or reach a climax after a fairly long middle section. The middle of the dance is too long when the onlooker loses sight of the beginning and does not recognize the end. How the beginning, middle and end share the total time duration of the dance is the composer's decision.

There are no set criteria for success in this respect. Each dance demands a different length of time.

– *The Dance Design in Space* –

The composer must also be concerned that the dance, which exists in space, uses space in a constructive and interesting way.

First, it should be decided how much space to use, relative to the idea and the space available. Second, a decision is made about where the front is, if it is not a stage space, or from which angles the dance will be seen to the best advantage. Then there are three further considerations:

1) the dancer's shape in space
2) the pathways created on the floor
3) the pathways created in the air

THE DANCER'S SHAPE IN SPACE

The dancer's shape in space creates a visual enhancement of the idea behind the movement. The dancer's *feeling* of shape through the kinesthetic sensation of the movement is a very important aspect of presentation of the dance to an audience.

'Feeling' a still shape can cause a sensation of movement and, unless the composer wishes to use absolute stillness for its own sake, every momentary pause or hesitation which retains body shape should create an illusion of movement. This is done by the dancer's feel of stretch, contraction or rotation continuing on into the space or into, or around the body, and by the dancer's focus. The movement in a body shape either lives or dies and the composer should be aware of each body shape as part of the material content which communicates the idea.

The dancer also makes shapes with his/her body as it moves and the onlookers see these shape images transmitted as part of the total expression. Therefore, they need to be clearly defined in movement. Extension and control of the dancer's movement in space are technical necessities for success in this respect.

AESTHETIC QUALITY OF SHAPE IN SPACE

The audience might also enjoy the aesthetic qualities the shapes may embody. If this is to be the case the composer must pay attention to the alignment of the dancer in relation to the front. The body which faces front with the arms and legs on a forward and backward plane loses its shape and line for the audience. It is vital that the perspective and directional implications of placement in relation to the view are considered. (Photos, 5, 6 below)

PATHWAYS CREATED ON THE FLOOR AND IN THE AIR

The pathways the dance creates on the floor and in the air are living parts of the dance. Curved air and floor pathways create feelings opposed to those which straight air and floor pathways provoke. Most dances have both straight and curved pathways and these can be presented in interesting ways.

The more formal symmetric patterns on the floor may be matched with similar patterns in the air, or vice versa, or, more asymmetric pathways on the floor may be amalgamated with

5 Wrong alignment

6 Right alignment

symmetric air pathways or vice versa. To make a symmetric floor or air pattern one would repeat lines or curves on the other side of the body or stage space so that the pattern is evenly distributed. To make an asymmetric floor pattern one would not be concerned to repeat particular lines or curves (see opposite).

Some composers may actually map out a floor pathway for the dance before composing the movement. This might ensure that the dance makes the fullest use of the space and with interesting patterns. On the other hand, in order to guide the emergence of floor and air patterns, some composers would prefer to create the movement by using their natural space patterning inclinations and the spatial characteristics inherent in movement content. Whichever way it is done, the composer should aim to make the spatial design of the dance visually stimulating.

The use of space is further defined by the spatial character-istics of the movements themselves, their level, size, direction and extension.

– *Motif in Composition* –

The dance composer, composing for a soloist, is concerned that:

1) the idea is established through the movement content which is organised into motifs, developments and variations;
2) there is enough repetition to confirm the movement images but that repetition is effected in different ways to maintain the onlooker's interest; and
3) the time and space aspects are interesting and varied and enhance the meaning.

The initial and succeeding motifs, which emerge through the composer's creative response to the stimulus, act as the catalytic agents for the rest of the dance work. If the motifs are 'right' in content and form, the dance stands a chance of being successful.

Symmetric floor pathways   Asymmetric floor pathways

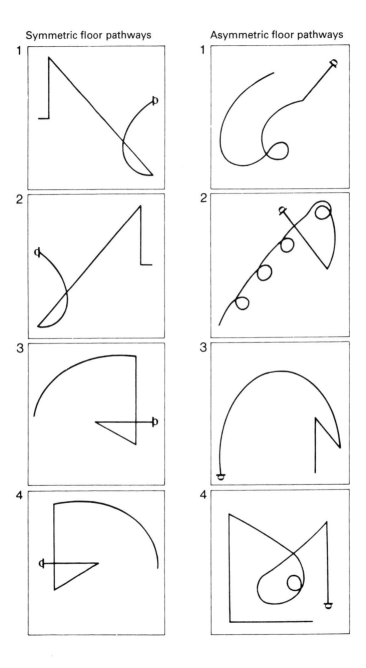

Methods of Construction 3
Motif into Composition for a Group

– *The Group as an Expressive Element* –

A group dance can be likened to an orchestral portrayal of music. Each of the dancers in the group has a vital part to play in the harmonious, living whole.

NUMERICAL CONSIDERATIONS
The composer should give careful consideration to the number of dancers needed for every one must contribute to the interpretation of the idea. There are certain expressive connotations which can be related to numbers. For instance, three people always suggest relationship of 2–1. An uneven number of dancers in the group can suggest the isolation of one to induce some kind of conflict, whereas an even number of dancers in the group can unite harmoniously or suggest symmetry and uniformity. Whatever the intention, the composer should be aware of these inherent connotations, though there can be exceptions. A trio, for instance may well be in harmonious relationship throughout the dance.

PLACEMENT AND SHAPE OF THE GROUP
The spatial placing and shape of the group has an effect upon the meaning of the movement. A circle facing inwards suggests unity of purpose excluding all focus from the outside world, whereas the same circle facing outwards, without contact, would imply outer interest and non-unity, or, if contact remained, a combination of inner and outer interest. A line, side by side and square on to the front can mean solidarity and unity, whereas a file has sequential connotations.

Consider, also, the expressive nature of a close mass of dancers as opposed to scattered individuals; a large square group opposed to scattered individuals; a large square group opposed to a small circular group; a circle with one dancer in the centre; a wedge or arrowhead shaped group; a group with a single individual apart; a group linked by physical contact; two groups of the same size facing each other. There are endless numerical and placement possibilities in group composition but the meaning of the dance is portrayed by its movement content which either supports or negates these natural numerical, placement and shape expressive implications.

– *Motif, Development and Variation* –

Once the composer has established how many dancers to use and how to group and place them, he/she has then to decide how to orchestrate the movement content for the group. A motif may be established by the whole group in unison which then needs repetition and development so that its meaning becomes clear.

The same possibilities of repetition through development and variation of the motifs exist for the group dance as for the solo (see Table 3 overleaf). Also, an important feature of duo or group composition is the possibility of presenting developments and variations of the movement content at *the same moment in time.* This can be achieved in action, for example, by one person or small group using the other side of the body, or a different body part, or by some members adding other actions to the motif, such as turn and travel. Developments and variations in action, quality, and use of space by the group can be presented as an interesting orchestration of movement content in time and space in the following ways:

– *The Time Aspect* –

	UNISON	CANON
a)	same movements	same movements
b)	complementary movements	complementary movements
c)	contrasting movements	contrasting movements
d)	background and foreground movements	background and foreground movements

UNISON

'In unison' means that the dance movement takes place at the same time in the group and there are four possibilities of presenting unison.

TABLE 3

How to achieve repetition of movement content through development and variation of motifs in duo or group composition

ACTION
1. Action by doing the same again in unison or canon

2. Action through use of the other side of the body or different body parts

3. Action through addition in action (turn, weight transference, travel, gesture, jump, stillness)

4. Action through extraction of action (part of the movement motif against the whole)

5. Action by changing the body flow, (one group successive another simultaneous)

QUALITY

1. Time–speed constrast within the group

2. Timing–canon–overlapping–sequence

3. Quality variation in Time, or Weight, or Flow, or a combination of these factors within the group

REPETITION through development and variation of

SPACE
1. Design by exact copy or complementing to achieve line repetition, or pathway repetition or shape repetition, or a combination of these

2. Space patterning within the group through variation of:
size
level
direction
extension
pathway

RELATIONSHIP

1. Relationship; numerical, placement and group shape variations

2. Juxtapositioning of movement content with the motif or motifs

a) Unison: all performing the same movements at the same time. The motif statement is reinforced by sheer multiplicity of number. If there are about twelve dancers, the communication is more forceful than if there are only two or three. This kind of unison is useful as a start in that the audience has only one movement motif to watch and can identify it quickly and, subsequently, follow the intricacies of its development within the group. Also, it may be that the composer uses all the dancers to create the climax. Unison can be made visually interesting by half the group emphasising one side of the body whilst the other half emphasises the other side.

b) Unison with complementary movements: this implies that movement in the group is occurring at the same time but that the parts of the group are not using identical movement. To complement means to *fill out* or *make more of* and this, in the context of a group dance, may mean that while one part of the group takes the original basic motif, the other part complements it, and therefore develops it. This can be done by emphasising a different body part, or performing on a different level, in a different direction, with a different amount of extension in space, or by slightly changing all the elements of the motif. By this means, the spectator should be able to appreciate simultaneous repetition of the motif which makes visual re-emphasis of the communication.

c) Unison with contrasting movements: this suggests that all movement takes place at the same time yet the smaller groups within the total group are performing contrasted movement patterns. A few dancers may be taking slow gentle arm gestures while others are doing fast accented foot patterns. This moment in the composition may introduce a new motif in contrast to the original, while the first is still in view. For dramatic purposes, the differences in the movement of the groups may be highlighted. This latter example is quite forceful in presenting opposing material content but it cannot be sustained for long, as it takes a great deal of concentration on the part of the viewer to absorb two simultaneous happenings.

d) Unison with background and foreground: this implies that one part of the group takes on the principal role while the rest of the group moves as a background, subordinate to, and supporting the main part. The dancers in the background might constantly repeat an extract of the motif while those in the foreground present the whole motif, or the background might move very slowly to give the effect of a moving backcloth enhancing the main motif.

CANON

'In canon' means that one part is followed by another in time. The actual amount of time that one part of the group is in front of another can be varied. For instance, one group could start a movement phrase and another group be one moment or several moments behind in time with the same phrase, or maybe, the phrase is only repeated by the second group after it is completed by the first group. The consecutive groups can come in at any time during, or after the initial phrase.

illustrates this point.

The sequence in canon can be started by one person and increase in number, or started with a number of people and decrease in number.

Continuous canon gives a sequential effect which may well be a feature of part of a group dance when the dancers take it in turn to do a movement or movement phrase. Single movement canon followed by a phrase canon can add interest to the time aspect of a group dance.

a) Canon with the same movements: the composer may wish to restate the motif by using a small part of the group immediately after the whole group, or he/she may wish to have a short motif repeated in the round-like fashion by several small groups taking turns. Individual dancers within the group could take turns or overlap while performing the same movement content.

b) Canon with complementary movements: this is known as 'question and answer', where one part of the group makes a statement and this is followed by another part of the group making a complementary movement response. The response could overlap, or follow the initial statement.

c) Canon with contrasting movements: here the groups take it in turns or overlap with contrasting movement. The composer may wish to establish two groups in turn and utilise contrasting movement patterns to emphasis their difference.

d) Canon with background and foreground movements: the composer could perhaps establish the background (like a bass introduction to a piece of music) and then bring in the foreground (or melody) during the background movement or immediately after it. The background movement could be used intermittently to punctuate the foreground.

The composer should attempt to use as many of these time aspect variations as are relevant to the idea. By such means, he/she can introduce and repeat the movement content, through

THE TIME ASPECT

	= a movement motif
	= complementary material
	= contrasted material
	= continuous background
	= intermittent background

development and variation, in unison or canon, in an interesting way within the group. The composer must consider the design of the total length of the dance and the allocation of time for the beginning, middle and end. *Methods of Construction 2* dealt with this aspect. Further discussion on the time design of the overall dance form will continue in *Methods of Construction 4.*

– *The Space Aspect* –

ORCHESTRATION OF GROUP MOVEMENT IN SPACE

The composer must consider the space aspects to achieve a relatedness of the group throughout the duration of the dance. If the movement were stopped at any moment during the dance, the relationship of the dancers should be as apparent as a visual picture. Dance is a visual art. The composer is producing pictures which range from being fleeting in nature to moments of stillness. There are numerous momentary pictures in a dance and even though the movement may not be stopped, these could be appreciated for their visual design.

8 Copying in opposition

7 Copying

9, 10 Complementary

11, 12 Contrasting

THE VISUAL DESIGN OF BODIES

The visual design satisfies the onlooker if relationship can be seen. Through perception of the designs of individual members of the group, and groups within the group, the viewer sees this relationship through *exact copy, complementary or contrasting designs.* Exact copy or complementary relationship is made apparent through repetition of line or shape. Contrast can be achieved by some members of the group taking different lines and shapes. In viewing a group dance, therefore, repetition and/or contrast can be seen to exist in space during each moment of time.

VISUAL DESIGN AS MEANING

The lines and shape each dancer creates with his/her own body in space and through space can be related to those of other dancers, either copying, complementing or contrasting, and this visual picture creates a momentary image which holds meaning for the onlooker (photos 7–12). A group of dancers emphasising curved body shapes and creating curved pathways in the air and on the floor gives a feeling of rounded, harmonious melodic relationship. This could be contrasted with another group creating straight, angular body shapes, moving in straight lines, which might give a feeling of inter-personal, disciplined and regimented relationship. It is repetition or contrast of the lines and shapes, as well as actions, of the dancers which makes a statement clear. Definition of the group shape in space through such means adds to the statement.

VISUAL DESIGN AS AN AESTHETIC QUALITY

Relationship of lines and shapes in space should make the dance a pleasure to view – an aesthetic experience. It is like standing back to view a beautiful cathedral. The 'architectural' design of the bodies, using repetition of line and shape in complementary or opposing directions in relation to the environment, can give a harmonious, pictorial effect to the audience. If, on the other hand, discord were the aim the composer would try to eliminate repetition in design at the moment it is to be portrayed.

For the solo dancer or individual members of the group, repetition and contrast of line and shape in the body are also an important aspect. The use of the arms complementing leg shape, the head following the line of the trunk, or the whole body making a shape by virtue of repetition in shape of its multiple parts, or one side to the body contrasting the other, illustrate how the design might add to the aesthetic quality of the dance (see photos 13, 14, 15, overleaf).

DESIGN OF THE SPACE

The composer not only has to consider the bodily design of the dancers and groups in space but also the design or shaping of the space itself.

Shaping the space is done by: (a) creating distance or space between members of the group, and (b) by virtue of movement through space.

DISTANCE OR SPACE BETWEEN

The whole of the stage space is available to the dance composer. He/she has to decide how much of it to use and how to use it in relation to the idea.

As soon as two dancers, or two groups, separate, space is created between them and it becomes a living element of the dance expression. If the distance between two groups is too great the composer has destroyed the relevance of the space between, as the audience cannot maintain both moving parts in vision. The nature of the space between is made apparent by the movement content and the dancers' focus – whether it is bonding the two groups, creating a void, or has equal pull from both sides.

As discussed at the beginning of this section, the placing of the dancers or groups in relation to each other suggests meaning. This placing also exposes patterns in space which should be varied as much as possible, within the context of the idea, so that the dance becomes an exciting visual experience for the viewer.

THE PATHWAYS CREATED BY MOVEMENT

The designs the dance reveals are not only defined by the distance between dancers and groups, but movement itself creates spatial pathways. The design which can be visualised by the audience in retrospect is defined by the movement over the floor and in the air. This is temporal spatial design. The composer should endeavour to make it as interesting as possible and keep it a living and inherently expressive part of the total expression.

13, 14, 15, Repetition of line and shape in the body

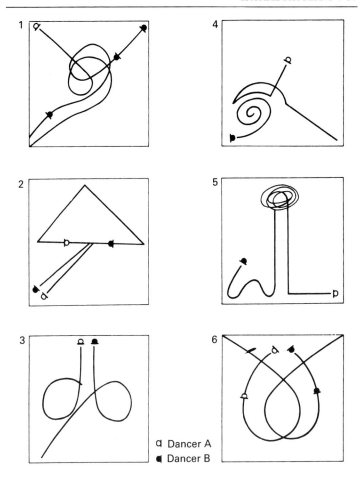

ɑ Dancer A
◄ Dancer B

A sequence of spatial patterns created by movement of two dancers over the floor

– *Motif into Composition for a Group* –

TO CONCLUDE

The dance composer who is working for a group, or within a group, is concerned that:

1) the idea is established through the movement content which is organised into motifs, developments and variations;
2) there is enough repetition both in the present and as part of the time construct; repetition in the present is seen in the design of each dancer or group in relation to the others and in the simultaneous developments and variation of motifs within the group; repetition as part of the time construct is seen through repetition of design or group shape in canon and development and variation of motifs in canon;
3) the orchestration of the group in time and space is interesting and varied and enhances the meaning behind the dance and makes it a rich visual experience for the onlooker.

Methods of Construction 4
The Dance Form

DESIGN IN TIME

The composer seeking form for the dance should consider that he/she is creating a design in time. This could be called a time picture. Like any picture it is built up from parts. Once the overall meaning is apparent, the parts fit into a shape or *form* which supports them. An analogy to architectural design illustrates this point. Each part of a building must blend into the whole. Even though each can be viewed for itself, it is its relationship with the other parts that gives it meaning. The gables, archways and turrets, for instance, fit into the overall structure defining its shape and style.

Architectural design is static – we can see it all at once. On viewing a dance, however, we can only perceive one piece at a time and we have to put the pieces together in our minds to form a picture of the whole. Since the experience lasts through time, it demands that the dance composer makes the dance pieces by dividing time.

The motif is used as a structural basis for the form. There will nearly always be more than one motif, and different outcomes from each motif must somehow merge into the whole mass with clarity and significance. The motifs themselves create time pictures by the movement which lasts an amount of time, has changing intensities and accents, pauses and stops.

MOVEMENTS AND MOVEMENT PHRASES

The beginning motif has in it a 'word', or a few 'words', giving a clue to the meaning of the whole. The motif may last in time just as a single 'word' or as a long 'sentence'. If it is the latter it is considered a movement phrase, which has a shape and logical time picture.

The phrase may start by dynamic, shouting, climactic movement and tail off to a calmer ending, or vice versa, or, build up to an explosive middle part and calming down end. So the phrase is structured into a *rhythmic pattern*. The next phrase could take on a different rhythm using the same movement again, but developed, in a different order. Each consecutive phrase makes clearer the idea by re-emphasising the same point, exposing a different view of the same thing, unfolding more content to support the point or even contrasting it by an opposite to give emphasis to the meaning.

SECTIONS

Phrases are usually bound together into sections. A section in a dance may be described as a collection of phrases which are connected – possibly derived from the first phrase which forms the motif, or made up from the inter-relationship of two phrase motifs. A new section would appear with the introduction of new material.

RHYTHM AND FORM

Movements, phrases and sections making patterns in time are some aspects of the rhythm of the dance. From this, it follows that every movement has rhythm. The energy which starts the movement, keeps it going and stops it, is given rhythmic shape by application and release of force within its duration of time. The force, or accents, punctuate and divide the time. Going back to the previous examples – a strong quick accent may begin the movement and then it may become slower and less strong to finish in a dying-away manner,

or the build-up could come in the middle of the movement or phrase,

or the end of the movement or phrase may become the most forceful giving a climax to the whole.

Interrelation of the time and weight factors provide the dance composer with a vast range of rhythmic possibilities.

The time picture created in the dance may be symmetrical with the force or accent appearing at regular intervals. This is known as a metric arrangement where the time between the accents is measured out evenly. It can be matched with musical measurements in time, e.g., $\frac{4}{4}$. Each metre of time lasts for the same duration, but rhythmic variation can occur within each (see diagrams opposite).

An asymmetric measurement of time is sometimes called breath rhythm. Here the measurements between accents are not even. The movement phrase has its own rhythm, the commas and full stops coming arbitrarily with the natural feeling of the phrase.

Some Divisions of Time in $\frac{4}{4}$

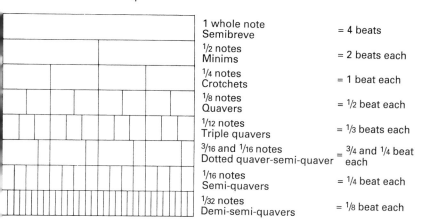

1 whole note Semibreve	= 4 beats
1/2 notes Minims	= 2 beats each
1/4 notes Crotchets	= 1 beat each
1/8 notes Quavers	= 1/2 beat each
1/12 notes Triple quavers	= 1/3 beats each
3/16 and 1/16 notes Dotted quaver-semi-quaver	= 3/4 and 1/4 beat each
1/16 notes Semi-quavers	= 1/4 beat each
1/32 notes Demi-semi-quavers	= 1/8 beat each

Various rhythmic arrangements within the time duration of 4 beats

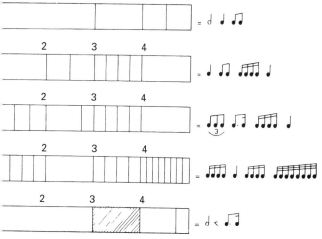

ORGANISATION OF THE FORM

The organisation of time and force in relation to each movement (whether it is quick, slow, accelerates, decelerates; has strong or light accents at the beginning, in the middle, or at the end of it; or increases or diminishes in force throughout its duration) and the organisation of these movements into phrases and sections determines the nature of the dance form. The style and quality of each movement motif will perhaps determine contrasting sections or sections which grow one from the other. The composer then has to consider the *ordering of the sections into a form or design in time.*

There are many ways of organising the form, and each dance should have its own unique structure but, because music is often used as accompaniment and dictates the overall form, musical forms have long been recognised frameworks into which dances are classified whether with musical accompaniment or not. These include Binary, Ternary, Rondo, Theme and Variations, and Fugue arrangements.

BINARY FORM

Binary form is commonly used in dance composition. The first section A is contrasted by a new section B, but the two have a common thread which binds one to the other like brother and sister. Each section may have contrasting elements, but there must be something similar in nature too. Perhaps the movement in section A is predominantly slow and gentle and that in section B, fast and strong, but the action patterns or spatial shape may be the same or similar. On the other hand, maybe it is only the dance idea that binds them together, each section taking a different aspect of the idea, but in this case too, there must be something else that relates them – perhaps the style of movement.

TERNARY FORM

Ternary form A.B.A is a conventional and satisfying form because going back to the beginning 'rounds it off'. Somehow this produces a comfortable and pleasant 'knew what was going to happen' feeling in the onlooker. The return to section A can be achieved by exact repetition of the initial section, or by reversing, highlighting parts, changing a few elements and changing the order of elements. They must, however, be very closely akin whilst the B section forms the contrast.

RONDO FORM

Rondo form A.B.A.C.A.D.A and so on, provides the composer with a verse and chorus framework which gives room for variation in the verses and development in the choruses. Variation can produce something new each time, but it must still have enough of the original to be considered a related part to the whole. Development can recall the origin in many ways without changing the essence. Again, this is a conventional and satisfying form to watch providing it is interesting enough. The onlooker can quickly identify the chorus movement and enjoy its repetition. (It is like enjoying a song chorus.) Through feeling a kinesthetic sympathy with the dancer, the onlooker can 'join in'.

THEME AND VARIATIONS

Theme and variations is a freer, more asymmetric and exciting form. The theme provides the basis for the variations. This is often called a sequential form in that the initial statement is followed by a number of developments or variations. The initial statement is not made again, and each variation becomes a basis for the next variation. Therefore the dance can finish with movement which is very different from that of the beginning. It is like watching a film when you do not know how it is to end. The composer has a freedom but must pay attention to connectedness throughout. Even if the initial movement phrase is not repeated, something of its nature should linger in the mind of the onlooker so that, on reflection, he/she appreciates the range of variations which have emerged.

CANON OR FUGUE

Canon or fugue is a composition in which one or two themes, or motifs, are repeated or initiated by successive dancers. These would then be developed in continuous interweaving of parts into a well-defined single structure. Dance studies in groups can usefully employ this form.

NARRATIVE FORM

Narrative form is not derived from musical form. The word narrative suggests that there is to be a gradual unfolding of a *story* or *idea.* The movement content is sequentially arranged into sections, A.B.C.D.E.F.G, etc., and each section is a further exposure of the idea or story.

If the dance conveys a series of images on one idea, the composer has the problem of linking sections so that each naturally flows into the next in a logical sequence. If the dance tells a story (dance-drama) the composer should make the parts adhere very closely. The sections in it should not always be apparent to the onlooker, although the composer may well find it useful to consider it section by section to ensure that there is richness, contrast, and variation in each part of the whole.

TO CONCLUDE

The above forms appear cut and dried and easy to distinguish one from the other. However, many dances are not true to the conventional forms and may be an amalgamation. For instance, a dance may start with an A.B.A form shape, and then go on

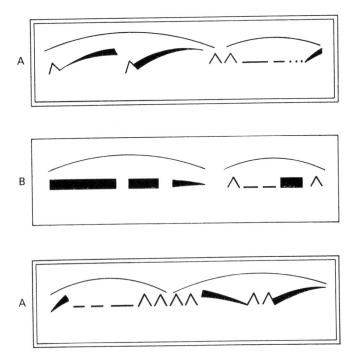

with C.D and back again to A; or may follow rondo form, but each new section could follow on narrative lines whilst the A section remains a chorus.

There are numerous possibilities open to the composer in the arrangement of the overall form. The essential thing to remember is that each part of the dance must have relevance to the whole.

It might be useful to think of a dance having outer and inner rhythmic forms. The inner rhythmic form consists of the time/force shape that each movement, movement phrase and section create, while the outer rhythmic form consists of the shape brought about by the juxtaposition of each section in the dance.

In the illustration opposite it can be seen that each movement has a rhythm, each of the phrases has a different rhythmic structure, and that the overall shape has an A.B.A rhythm – the B section forming a contrast to both As.

=======

Methods of Construction 5
Elements of Construction

Several elements of construction have already emerged in the discussion on the construction of a dance. It may be useful to convey these in a list so that the reader can select each element and evaluate its constructional purpose in any given dance:

1) the motif/s (foundation/s of construction)
2) repetition
3) variation and contrasts
4) climax or highlights
5) proportion and balance
6) transition
7) logical development
8) unity

Each of these elements could be discussed in relation to many forms of art. Each element is related to, and complements, the others. All serve unity which is the overall aim in any art. To achieve unity the other seven elements must be employed.

THE MOTIF/S OR FOUNDATION/S OF CONSTRUCTION

In *Methods of Construction 2 and 3*, we have discussed the function of the motifs in composition in some depth. It remains to say that these dominant elements of the composition only emerge as dominant in the light of all the other constructional devices used.

* Without repetition, the motifs would be forgotten.
* Without variation and contrast, repetition of the motifs would be dull if presented ad lib in their original form.
* A dance lacking climax or highlights would seem to have motifs which have no content worth highlighting.
* Without careful proportioning and balancing of the whole work each of the motifs could become almost eliminated or even too dominant.
* Without transitions the motifs would be isolated movement statements. Transitions between movements within the motif and between the motifs are important in defining the phrase and section shaping of the dance.
* Without logical development from motif to motif the theme of the dance would be blurred.

The motifs contain the main ingredients which provide the unifying threads for the whole work. These include the style, qualitative colour, light and shade, line and shape in space, and types of action which motivate the rest of the work.

REPETITION

From the preceding text, repetition must be recognised as a main device in dance composition. It should be clear that repetition in a dance exists in the form of development and variation of the movement material which is established within each motif. Also that, in the context of dance as an art form, the word repetition has wider interpretations than its normal usage.

VARIATION AND CONTRASTS

These elements of construction differ but complement each other. Variation demands that the content, which has already been established in the dance, is *used again* in a different way. Contrast demands the introduction of *new* material either within the original motif during a repetition, or as a variation of the motif. The new material can be another motif of course.

A successful dance should feature both these elements. Variation gives an interesting logical development to the whole providing the necessary means for repetitions of the theme, so that the audience can view it in different ways with growing understanding. Contrasts provide the exciting changes which colour the dance and stand out as points of reference in relation to the total material content. Contrasts can be effected in many ways, and often – though not always – provide the climaxes or highlights in a dance.

To make a contrast, the composer should consider a change in content but this should not be done for the sake of contrast alone. It must also be relevant to the idea behind the dance. In quality content, for instance, the slow section could be followed by a fast section, or the predominantly slow section could have a fast movement to break the continuity of slowness. In spatial content predominantly small low level movements could be contrasted by a large high level movement. In action a phrase containing stepping, gesturing and travelling could be contrasted by jumping; a phrase using one side of the body could be contrasted by one movement of the other side; predominantly symmetrical body action could be followed by a sudden change to asymmetric use of the body.

Contrast is not only achieved through sudden changes in content. It is possible to build gradually towards a contrast. Movement might accelerate from slow into quick, show little tension and increase in strength to show a great deal of tension, start low and gradually grow to high level and so on. Contrast emerges as contrast if the predominant material content is interrupted or punctuated by fresh or opposing movements. It would seem that the opposite, or near opposite, in content is a requisite feature of contrast.

CLIMAX OR HIGHLIGHTS

Many people think that a dance should have only one climax, the rest of the material content supporting it. In fact, a dance can have many highlights which may or may not be real climaxes too. In retrospect, the moments which are remembered are highlights of the dance and remain of special significance to each particular viewer. In a work of art, no two people view in the same way, and no two people would necessarily agree on the highlight moments in a dance. If, however, these moments come to fruition in one big climax and this is the intention of the composer, then everyone should see and agree that this is *the* climax. It depends upon the nature of the dance and the idea whether there is one climax or several climaxes or whether these are merely highlights without the especially noticeable features of a 'super' climax. These latter features may emerge with a sudden attack, or build up slowly to an explosive moment. For instance, if the dance has been earthbound and gestural, a sudden series of leaps accompanied by the trunk twisting, bending and stretching will make a contrast which is also a climax. On the other hand, a climax could be seen as the ultimate development of a motif. In all events, if it is a real climax it should stand out very prominently. Highlights appear like little sparks of interest, and exist through the composer's exposition of artistic, skilled and beautifully conceived movement ideas which stand out as such to the onlooker.

Some of the means by which climaxes or highlights can be achieved in movement are illustrated in Table 4 opposite.

PROPORTION AND BALANCE
These are complementary elements of construction. Proportion refers to the size and magnitude of each part in relation to the whole, and balance refers to the equilibrium of content within each of these proportionate parts and the whole.

The proportion of one part of a dance in relation to its other parts has to be right. Equal proportioning of parts may become too boring. It is all too easy to go on developing for too long with one motif or statement or conversely, make too little of a section of movement content thereby losing its significance through lack of repetition. Each part of a dance should be only as long as is necessary. There is no easy answer for a perfect proportion of parts in any dance. It is an intuitive feeling for 'rightness' that guides the use of this element of construction.

Similar comments can be made in reference to balance. Here the composer must be aware of the balance which exists in the *choice* of movement content within one part of the dance in relation to the choice in another. Within the range of material that the composer deems suitable for the total dance, it is important to consider the proportionate use so that the whole is balanced. A beginning 'packed with delights' and then trailing away to an uninteresting end is unbalanced, whereas a dance

TABLE 4

Some ideas on how climax or highlight might be achieved

ACTION

1. Special emphasis on one or a few actions within the motif through:
   a) repetition
   b) enlargement by means of development
   c) defined by stillness before or after the action/s

2. Change in action content

3. Interesting development or variation through addition of action content

QUALITY

1. Sudden or subtle change of qualities

2. Build up in force or time or both

   Sudden accents-short continuous dynamic passages

3. Repetition of rhythmic pattern-change of rhythmic pattern

4. Contrast in flow

CLIMAX OR HIGHLIGHT through

SPACE

1. Sudden or subtle change or contrast in:
   a) amount of space used,
   b) placing in space,
   c) focus in space,
   d) space pattern – size, level direction, pathway

2. Special enlargement or development of the spatial aspects of the motif

RELATIONSHIP

1. Variation or contrast of group relationship

2. Addition in number moving
   Subtraction in number moving

3. Particular juxta-positioning of the movements within the motifs, phrases or sections

which has its contrasts, climaxes or highlights, repetitions and variations in movement content spaced out throughout its duration may well be judged as a balanced form and should succeed in sustaining interest. The composer's aim is to achieve equilibrium of parts so that a unity becomes apparent. For instance, the gentle flowing parts of the dance should not be made insignificant in relation to the strong dominant parts. The section of the dance performed by a soloist should stand as significant in juxtaposition with the section in which a large group performs. All parts must enhance the idea and be inseparable from the whole.

In a more specific sense, the proportion element of construction could refer to how many dancers are performing and the proportionate divisions within the number. The balance element could refer to where they are in relation to each other and the space. (Some detail on this is included in *Methods of Construction 3*.) It is important that proportion of numbers is relevant and enhances the dance idea, and that these must change in order to keep it an interesting feature. Similarly, the balance and placing of the groups in relation to each other have expressive significance. The arrangement and placing of dancers and props in the stage space are governed by a need for symmetric or asymmetric balancing which is determined by the composer's treatment of the theme. The composer should also consider the proportionate use of the stage space to give a balanced effect within the environment.

TRANSITION
The composer must use this element of construction to link all the parts and effectively create a whole. Transitions are very important and perhaps the most difficult aspects of the composition.

There are no set ways of making transitions from one part of a dance to another. The composer usually works on these in an intuitive way. Finding an answer to a movement problem can only be achieved by moving through all the possible avenues until it feels and looks right.

Transitions can be a very short or quite long in time. Indeed a transition from one part to another may be effected by merely *holding still* in a body position before moving into the new part. This has the effect of holding on to something for a second or two whilst an impression is formed by the audience before changing the subject. Or, the transition may be made as a *hesitation* between movements or phrases or as *anticipation* of movement to follow – for example, a lean of the body into a direction before actually travelling on that pathway. Transitions hold parts together by bridging and, therefore, help to create the overall rhythmical framework. The longer transition, lasting perhaps as long as a *phrase*, usually acts as a link between sections.

The subtle transitions from one position to another, and the more obvious transitions from one section of the dance to another, all play an important tying-together role. Movement tied to movement should be logical, clear and, above all, appear easily performed. Movements of a transition between sections should, perhaps, have a lingering flavour of the preceding section and act as an introductory passage to the succeeding section.

LOGICAL DEVELOPMENT

Logical development becomes apparent by virtue of repetition, climax, transition, contrast and variety in the dance. When we speak of logical development, we refer to the natural growth of the dance from its beginning to its end. If something is logical it also has meaning and 'raison d'être' throughout its existence. The beginning of the dance starts a line of thought for the onlooker and from this, ideas offshoot in many directions, while all retain a common thread. The common thread is the basis upon which logical development depends, and is more than just the idea, story or motivational stimulus of the dance. The common thread is initiated through the beginning motif which is a *movement interpretation* of the motivation or idea behind the dance. This movement interpretation has an identity in terms of action, qualities, space and perhaps relationships. The rest of the dance, or a part of the dance, discloses more of this identity through repetition, variation and contrast. The pursuit of form created from the identity of the foundational motifs determines logical development. In this way all the movements appear relevant and part of the growth of the dance. The climaxes are in the right places and have the right kind of initiation to fulfil their purpose. The whole leads perfectly to its end which seems right as an outcome. Not inevitable, but right. In fact the end of a dance is probably the most important part. If the end fails – the dance fails.

To summarise: logical development of the dance ensures unification whereby each part is linked to the common thread through the composer's movement interpretation of the idea. If the constructional elements of motifs, developments, variations, contrasts, climaxes or highlights, and above all transitions, are successfully employed, then the dance appears to have a logical development which in turn produces unity.

UNITY

This is the overall constructional element. The final shape that emerges when the dance is over is realised through unity. To make an analogy: if all the parts fit into the jigsaw puzzle it finally produces a whole picture within its round or square frame. The *movement content* with its inherent meaning and the way in which the *constructional elements* have been employed form the pieces of the jigsaw and its overall shape or dance form (e.g. Ternary form) forms the frame. The pieces knitted together become unified within the frame and also form the frame which produces unity. If even one piece is missing or does not fit then the whole never becomes a whole and unity is lost.

The dance composer must aim for unity. To understand how it is reached in a dance requires a good deal of experience and artistic awareness, but it can be recognised by laymen and even by children. Somehow a good dance is appreciated as an entity which has meaning and significance beyond the scope of its pieces. A dance which has the quality of unity is likely to be successful.

Methods of Construction 6
Style

UNDERSTANDING THE TERM 'STYLE'

In dance, the terms style and technique can mean one and the same thing because the word technique often means the content of the idiom, not merely how it is manipulated/presented. Thus we have ballet, jazz, contemporary techniques which produce these particular styles. For some, use of the word genre to describe the idiom or type of dance – ballet, jazz, contemporary – provides a solution since each can be articulated in many stylistic flavours. For example, a contemporary dance might be labelled jazzy in style, balletic or neo-classical, ethnic or as having a particular social dance flavour.

The word technique is also used in most dance contexts when discussing physical skill and, to a dancer, technique means acquiring skill through attending class, exercising the body and practising movements to achieve perfection. The class invariably is taken in one technique as opposed to another – i.e. to become skilled in ballet one goes to ballet classes. So at class level, the words technique and style often do mean the same thing. Genre is not yet a word in common usage.

It is interesting to study how new techniques, or changes of emphasis in traditional techniques, form particular styles. All choreographers try to invent new styles and even if a traditional style is used, rather than merely rearranging the prescribed content, the choreographer will probably take elements from the traditional style and embrace them within a style more relevant to the choreographer's own time.

Balanchine, as an example of a master classicist, abstracted the pure classical syntax of movement from ballet and developed it into modern-formalism. This term describes a style which has been created through a process of abstraction. From the traditional theatrical spectacle of ballet, Balanchine abstracted the 'bare-bones' austerity of ballet essence. In exploring the essence of ballet, Balanchine concentrated on the movement itself and particularly concerned himself with the phenomenon of grace. Technique was the means by which his dancers achieved the essential grace which, for Balanchine, was the essence of ballet. His particular ways of moving into and out of ballet positions and linking of movements created his style – the Balanchine style relevant to his time. His manipulation of the standardised technical elements of ballet was the outcome of a mixture of experiences – those early in his life in St Petersburg and with the Diaghilev company, those connected with twentieth-century modern expressionist dance styles and those connected with modern art in general and music in particular. Furthermore, the general style of American dancers with its broad, expansive and energetic characteristics similarly influenced his movement repertoire. All of these influences, and doubtless others, became absorbed and structured into a coherent Balanchine style.

Balanchine's ballets are prime examples of the changes in emphasis in ballet technique in that legs are extended very high, there is an accent on line and fluency, the torso is used to tip the body into and out of balances and the aspect of body design or shape is an apparent focus throughout his work to generate the quality of grace for its own sake. The style, therefore *creates* the expression of grace, the technique or content with its emphasis on line, shape, balance, etc., and the choreographic form with an emphasis on order, harmony and a pleasingly unified appearance, create the style of modern-formalism. Modern, because it is a twentieth-century development of a traditional style and formalism, because it focuses on form and movement for their own sake.

FACTORS AFFECTING STYLE

From the above brief discussion of Balanchine's style, it would appear relevant, in summary, to say that style is culturally and historically defined but, in dance as in other arts, it also has much to do with the technique employed. Graham's work is a clear example of how technique forms the basis of style and expression in dance and how this is formulated out of a need to find ways of expressing in a manner relevant to the time and place in which the art form finds itself.

Martha Graham's technique evolved first as a means of:

> expressing personal feelings and national identity through recognisable prototypes of character and movement and the abstraction of those feelings to a more cosmic level through the use of symbol, myth and psychoanalytic exploration.
>
> (Seigel, 1979), pp. 175–6

This stylised naturalism was typical of the 1930s period when Graham first started to choreograph. In a Graham dance people make statements. Most often these are dramatic and powerful. To effect this Graham's theatre dance style is distinguished by its unnaturalness. As Seigel says, 'Graham has always tried to formalise natural impulses, to abstract human feelings into a set expressive language'. This procedure was common in the 1930s when Freudian theory encouraged artists to explore new ways of expressing human feelings. As Jowitt states:

Graham likened herself, at a primitive stage in her development, to the dancer in a primitive culture ... She would start from scratch, concentrating on the pulse of the body, on the rhythmic action of the foot against the ground, and articulate the head, arms and hands as her work evolved ... breath was crucial – not so much everyday even-rhythmed breathing, but the gasp, the sob, the slow sigh of relief, and the ways in which these – heightened and abstracted – could affect the dancer's muscles and skeleton. Her theory of 'contraction and release' was built on the act of inhaling and exhaling. The dancer, whether sitting, standing, kneeling or lying down, caves in as if suddenly hit with a blow to the center of her body. But 'caves in' is the wrong term if that implies any relaxation of tension ... As Graham developed her technique, a contraction might hit the dancer sideways, make her twist, spiral, or be spun to the floor. It might attack percussively then deepen slowly, resonating throughout her body. But always, no matter how drastic the fall, there is release, a rise, an advance, an inhalation. The dancer waits – poised, charged – for the next crisis.   (1988) pp. 164, 166

Ideas like these created very individual styles of dance movement. Certainly, the Graham technique is idiosyncratic and as demanding and unnatural as classical ballet. However, the style and kind of expression most characteristic of Graham's work, seem no longer relevant to today's choreographers so the contemporary techniques used in dance works, though frequently derived from Graham's technique, have changed. It is interesting to note the similarity between ballet and contemporary dance here, in that it is common practice to take Graham classes, learning the Graham specified expressive language and perfecting a whole range of unnatural movement content and yet, in the performance of choreographers' works, never to use these movements in their original form. Hence, we see a definite division between the style of what is taught in technique class and what is required on stage. (It is acknowledged that the body instrument is superbly tuned and prepared for any dance co-ordination by virtue of the practice of Graham technique, but if the term technique refers to content for dance, the actual movement content is no longer relevantly expressive for today's choreographers.) Yet, the style of Graham's work remains, in essence, the hallmark of most of the contemporary theatre dance available to us. The styles of Graham, Cunningham and a few other early modern dance artists have become integrated and generalised to serve the needs of present-day choreographers.

This generalised contemporary dance style includes movements emphasising the use of the torso, feet in parallel, strict concern for body design and spatial design, movements of isolated parts of the body as well as the whole, emphasis on the pelvic region and the centre initiating and causing momentum, tension between up and down, floor-work and extensive variations of qualities and phrasing. The dance composer, through study of contemporary dance works on video or preferably in live theatre settings, will absorb the flavour of this generalised contemporary dance style and employ it as a basic stylistic source for his/her own dances.

Another important feature of the generalised style in main-stream dance choreography is the use of symbolic action embedded in a unified whole. This can be illustrated by reference to Jiri Kylian's work. In his dances based upon ideas the symbols are not literal and referential. The image is abstract and subtle in meaning. But his style of symbolising a theme is also very much integrated with his style of forming a dance and it is this aspect of his choreography which is masterful. One becomes delighted by the build-up, integration and development of motifs, the inventive way in which they are repeated within intricate patternings, the excitement of choreographic devices, such as canon, perfectly placed to make important moments stay in one's mind long after the dance is over, the intricacy, fluency and grace of the couples weaving around, over, through, towards and away from each other creating particularly pleasing spatial and rhythmic nuances. These are some of the ways in which Kylian's personal style becomes evident and some of the reasons why his works also, like Balanchine's, can be labelled as modern-formalism.

There is a recognisable look to Kylian's work as there is to Balanchine's and Graham's. Kylian, like other choreographers, attempts to move away from any such trademark. He said, 'I prefer to think I didn't have a style. I like to change my ways from ballet to ballet, but of course, you cannot avoid your own handwriting' (reported by Anna Kisselgoff writing in the *New York Times*, 1979).

So far then, in the contemporary dance context we have the current generalised dance technique style, the ways in which ideas are presented symbolically with a concentration on stripping away the dramatic literal gesture content to create subtle hints of the idea, and an emphasis on the form aspects of composition, all contributing to the overall style of dances. Added to this list, the following factors also affect style.

Each theme has stylistic properties intrinsic to it. For example, in Bruce's *Berlin Requiem*, 1982, we see the styles of the 1930s dance forms, characteristic poses and behaviours of the bar-frequenting social group, amalgamated with some movement characteristics of the films of the period. To embody the expression, these stylistic aspects of the theme are inextricably interwoven with a contemporary dance style and approaches to choreography as listed above. But, since Bruce has done the amalgamating and weaving of the parts into a unified whole, the result carries a powerful Bruce signature.

Hence, it appears that the style and expression of a dance work are likely to emerge as a compound of several elements, each of which has boundaries. The technique and kind (genre) of dance set one boundary. Added to these we have the personal style of the choreographer pervading the work. This comes over as a personal interpretation and way of using the technique, together with a personal interpretation of the idea and the conventions and meanings associated with it. So, we have the possibility of style within style, within style.

Yet another stylistic boundary derives from the current views on dance as a theatre art and the choreographer's attitude towards these. Clearly, both Bruce and Kylian are what might be labelled 'mainstream' choreographers – they use highly skilled dancers, they generally have themes to dance about, they create symbols abstracting the essence of the idea. Kylian concentrates on sheer dance quality, the theme instrumental to this, while Bruce gives greater emphasis to the emotional impact of the theme. But both aim for unity of form. They present the dance works so that the audiences can enjoy the intrinsic qualities of good dancing, line, shape, pattern, dynamic contrasts etc. Kylian emphasises formalism and the physical side of it, Bruce emphasises expressionism, but clearly both adhere to the mainstream view of dance.

Contrary to this, we have the post-modern or 'new dance' exponents who have formulated different views of dance as art. Here, the outcome is dependent upon how they see dance: as unconnected or fragmented movements in time and space, or as mathematically organised movement in time and space, or as natural everyday action for its own sake, or as spontaneous response to commands or improvised movement of others, or as informed happenings, or as exposure of social behaviours through realistic physical contact and body language which might otherwise be confined to private relationships (e.g. the DV8 Physical Theatre). However, these are not the only characteristics which result in these choreographers being collectively called post-moderns. In addition, they share characteristics such as the manner of working choreographically – by experimentation with little concern for rules or conventions – and the movement content – mostly natural, relaxed and showing little concern for shape, placement or focus in space and technically complex patterns of movement. These are some of the distinguishing features of the post-modern style/genre. Further in-depth discussion of post-modern/new dance can be found in *Methods of Construction 8.*

HOW TO STYLISE A DANCE

It is obvious, then, that the complexity of the concept of style demands that a composer understands what is involved in stylising a dance and that it cannot be left to chance if the dance is going to make an impact and 'stand the test of time'. While these might appear grandiose ideals for a student composer, it is always necessary to aim for originality if the created dance is to be valued. Copying the style of a known choreographer can be a useful learning process but ultimately, even if a dance is composed ' in the style of . . . ', it should bear the distinctive signature of the composer. No two people have exactly the same backgrounds, even if trained at the same time and in the same place they will perceive it differently because of their own different experiences. Moreover, interpretation of themes, use of techniques in movement and compositional form will vary from person to person. This is what is so special about art – each person's work is distinctive. Style is one of the features which makes for this distinction but it is also influenced by the cultural and artistic practices of particular times and places. It is the understanding of these practices that the student composer needs to develop so that the dances composed achieve both artistic relevance and originality.

The range and complexity of expression in dance today demand a complex mixing of tried and tested techniques and styles and a constant search for new ones. For example, a theme may require a social/contemporary dance style such as Twyla Tharp's *Sinatra Suite* (1977), a neo-classical style such as Jiri Kylian's *Sinfonietta* (1979), a physical theatre/contact improvisation style such as DV8's *Dead Dreams of Monochrome Men* (1988), an ethnically influenced style such as Christopher Bruce's *Ghost Dances* (1981). Whatever the theme the composer needs to research all aspects of its time/place i.e. the cultural characteristics, and search for the most appropriate technique/content and choreographic approach to express it. To do this it might be helpful to study ways in which the theme has been expressed before, if it has, so that the composer's choice of style is informed.

An ability to make such decisions implies a vast knowledge of techniques and styles and, of course, student composers do not often have more than one technique in their repertoire with its intrinsic style, be it ballet, contemporary or jazz, for example. In education, there is insufficient time to train young dancers to achieve mastery of skill in even one technique and it would be wrong to do this anyway because it immediately limits the style and kinds of expression to those which that particular technique can articulate. All techniques have such limitations.

It would seem that, in an ideal world, pupils in school and college should come to understand the significant differences in expression in a number of tried and tested techniques and styles so that they may selectively employ the right combinations of these in their own creative endeavours. Resource-based teaching/learning, the subject of the Section 3 in this book, is in my view the best way forward. A study of current and past repertoire of dance art works in the composer's own culture and outside it too has to be the means towards the end of developing an understanding of style and how to stylise a dance. This is how musicians learn about style – through listening to, studying and playing renowned pieces. Dance composers too need to work in this way – watch, study and perform snippets from dance works choreographed by professionals.

Methods of Construction 7
Improvisation in the Process of Composition

MEANING OF TERMS – IMPROVISATION AND EXPLORATION

First, it is important to discuss the meaning of the term 'improvisation' and its relationship with the term 'exploration' which is used frequently in this book. The latter is defined as a systematic investigation, examination, study, search with a view to making specific discoveries and learning about something. Improvisation, however, is defined as invention without preparation, to execute spontaneously in an impromptu or unforeseen way. (*Universal Dictionary, Reader's Digest*, 1987)

It would seem, however, that the dance community uses the term *improvisation* to cover the range of activity encapsulated in both these definitions. Mackrell (1992) in describing Butcher's *Landings* (1976), for example, states that:

> A lot of the movement was improvised in performance, though the structure of the piece was very carefully set.
>
> (p. 71)

Within the confines of the above definition, it might not be appropriate to describe this as true improvisation because the performer cannot respond entirely spontaneously; freedom is limited within a tightly structured piece.

Improvisation true to the definition above has been ascribed to the work of the X6 Collective by Jordan (1992):

> A strand of quiet, 'spiritual' work was made for a single showing . . . perhaps . . . as an opposition to the accreditable, repeatable products associated with establishment dance. Improvisation could be seen as directly oppositional in this sense. Here, in some cases, pleasure for the audience lay primarily in following the process of a performer's spontaneous response to the situation.   (p. 74)

Although, in comparison with the former, the latter example fits the definition of improvisation well, the term improvisation is used, in practice, in both and perhaps quite rightly so. After all, jazz musicians *improvise* when they create numerous variations on the original musical theme in their 'breaks' and the original constitutes tight structure.

The term exploration is clearly not appropriate here or in Mackrell's discussion of Butcher's work because the 'improvised' actions are occurring in performance, in real time, when it is not appropriate to undertake a 'systematic search'. Rather the dancer/musician lets imagination and spontaneity of response to the given structure take off in *impromptu, unforeseen ways.* The immediacy of performance makes a difference here. Conversely, one does not say that a visual artist is improvising with representation. The term exploration is fully appropriate in this case as it may be in the other non-temporal arts where there is time to consider and explore different ideas before selection. But we are discussing the process here, not the product.

In this process, of course, the choreographer, playwright or music composer explores and selects in this way in order to arrive at a final product. In the context of dance composition, Section 1 of this book focused on *exploration* as systematic searching for movement material with consideration of the possible implicit meanings. It is difficult to say exactly when the process of exploration becomes improvisation because exploration of an idea or range of movements is often effected *through* improvisation to examine the potential, to try out and feel practically, what is right.

However, the Mackrell and Jordan quotations above were not focused on the process of composing but on the products or dance compositions themselves. Clearly, improvisation occurs both in the process and in some products and it varies from being an open, free spontaneous response in movement to a more limited, framed and yet individual interpretation within a given structure. Hence, a broader definition of the term 'improvisation' is needed in a dance context.

In Section 2, *Methods of Construction 1*, such a broader definition was introduced in that the concept is described as 'varying between free and limited improvisation'. Here *improvisation* was discussed as a starting strategy in composition and ideas were offered on how movement might be selected from improvisation to structure the initial motif/s for the dance. It was also proposed that this selection might be guided by feeling (intuition), or by a process of objective evaluation through application of knowledge of the craft of composition. This consideration of improvisation led to the beginnings of composition (see page 30). However, improvisation is an ongoing process throughout the act of composing a dance.

This chapter therefore develops the concepts introduced earlier and then discusses possible roles for improvisation in the process of composition.

FREE AND LIMITED IMPROVISATION

The concepts of abandonment, of loss of directed thought, of free-flight imaginative indulgence are conjured up when one thinks of free and spontaneous improvisation. It seems to emerge from the sub-conscious levels, from a kind of trance-like immersion in feeling. Movement seems un-structured, open and uninhibited. Such improvisations produce new/fresh movements or treatments of themes. Yet like flights of fancy when half awake, it is not easy to recapture or remember the outcomes of free improvisations for composition purposes.

As soon as directed conscious thought comes into play, the improvisation becomes less free. Maybe this occurs most of the time in that compositions usually emerge from researched ideas for dances with perhaps some of the parameters clarified such as the accompanying music, the style, the storyline. Whatever is already in place, the structure has begun to take shape and improvisation is undertaken with some ideas, even if vague, as to what is appropriate for the dance.

So maybe there is not so much an either/or about improvisation for dance composition – either free or limited, but that ninety-five per cent falls into the category of limited improvisation and that the degrees of limitation vary from very little to a great deal.

On the other hand, all composers should experience improvisation towards the free end of the continuum and the accompanying sense of 'immersion' in some way. Even if guided only by music (which of course puts limitation on it), the enriching effect of such liberation and unrestraint will, in my view, have beneficial effects upon subsequent compositions, perhaps after a fair time gap. Such experiences, often very feelingful, somehow feed intuition and provide movement answers to problems in what might be described as insightful moments. This might be a flawed argument philosophically, but my experience has shown that some very original ideas come to the surface in free improvisation and they are not always lost in the memory's sub-conscious. A sensation or association of feeling with a certain movement idea can create clues as to the original improvised actions and, after work has been done on them, they might become realised and set into the composition. This might be described as moving from feeling to knowing – from spontaneity to discriminating selection. Hence, students should attempt to engage in free improvisation from time to time if only as a means of permitting imagination to fly and the unexpected movement to emerge. Some ways of experiencing this might be as follows.

a) Concentration on imagined feelings, emotions or situations as starting points for improvisation might be achieved if the students start by lying relaxed on the floor with eyes closed, and a 'story', full of potential movement responses, is spoken by the teacher. Listeners should allow the images to form and flow freely in their minds while the narrator takes them deeply into the feelings. In empathy with the feelings, the images will be movement based because the 'story' has been especially selected to evoke movement responses. The latter, however, should be achieved only by concentration on the feelings. There can be no suggestions about the movement outcomes since these should emerge without constraints on the students.

Students might listen to a passage of text about a political prisoner's ordeals and feelings during imprisonment (e.g. John McCarthy's). They should be invited to move when they feel inclined to or hold a still position in relation to their feelings about the story. The students will be led to concentrate fully on McCarthy's feeling of weight on his body with the ceilings and walls closing down and in on him, of fearful claustrophobia and sheer helplessness when gagged in a sack in the boot of a car – like a small baby, totally dependent on others to serve his needs. The 'story' might continue with McCarthy's feeling of false joy when released from the confined car boot and the taped gagging, only to be thrown into a bare concrete cell. Throughout the 'story' students should be focusing inwards and, when they move, the truth in their feelings should be apparent. If this is not the case, free improvisation has not occurred.

The next step might be to recall and develop some of the movement responses effected during the free improvisation and build ideas from these. This then shifts from free into limited improvisation.

b) It could be argued that the above is not really free improvisation since the 'story' limits the outcome. Perhaps the only way of getting into truly free improvisation is just to move in silence. This is not easy in a class situation since the students are bound to affect and infect each other as they move. However, a more experienced dance composer can beneficially work alone in this way. At first, no doubt, the same old movements will emerge but given time, patience and some taking of risks, new variations or combinations of these will develop too. It might be likened to a purging of oneself of old and clichéd vocabulary until something fresh and different becomes evident. From these movements which could be described as distantly related to the composer's vocabulary, there might be a few totally new movement ideas. Given a creative composer, these ideas may spark off yet more new movements.

The teacher can play an important role in the process of using such improvisations as a basis for composition. An observed 'lovely moment there – try to remember it, Michael' and similar encouraging comments addressing different members of the group might help students to note the imaginative, fleeting moments.

The next step might be to recall, then link these movements to emotions or ideas to find expressive potential. This association will probably drive the improvisation forward in a more structured way by virtue of limitations imposed by the idea. Even if there is no associated feeling or idea, the abstract movement content emerging from the free improvisation will put boundaries on subsequent movement ideas. The range of associations needs somehow to be explored before the movement idea is abandoned.

Rather than sacrificing this free improvisation for a more limited form which is bound to occur in any one ongoing session, it might be wise to leave gaps of time between free improvisations so that a freshness of approach in producing new movements is achieved each time. Whatever the process here, new movement content should be the outcome and this points to the real value of free improvisation for all dance composers.

Limited improvisation, as stated above, is the more usual approach in dance composition. Here, in my view, creativity can be greater than in a free improvisation situation because, with boundaries defined, there seems to be more depth to penetrate. This brings to mind the old maxim that total freedom is no

freedom at all, but it also suggests that such a view is contra-
dictory in the light of the above discussion on the value of free
improvisation. Perhaps it is a matter of experience. Beginner
dancers and composers may feel very inhibited by a total
freedom and will often not be able to move at all, whereas more
experienced dancers at least have learned vocabularies of dance
movement from which to start. On the other hand, a clean slate
or lack of preconceived ideas can permit more freedom. It is
difficult to be certain as to the benefits of extreme freedom for
beginner dance composers since some can let go without inhibi-
tion and produce very fresh, interesting movements untied to any
techniques, whilst others cannot get through a self-conscious
barrier. Maybe the teacher in this case should open up opportunities for free improvisation but be ready to put limitations in
place should the students seem lost as to what to do.

Beginner composers can learn how to improvise and therefore
gain confidence if set strict limitations. An example of this
might be as follows, but it is interesting to note that the act of
improvising is described as 'exploring'.

Exploration of individual action concepts – sway, sweep,
swing, pull, toss, swirl, rock, knock, fall and roll, and qualities
such as accelerate, decelerate, accent, freely go, suddenly stop
– could lead to the making of phrases using 'commas and full
stops' to depict images of gusts of wind at various strengths.
Each exploration requires improvisation in order that new and
various ways of throwing, for example, are experienced.

The improvisation at first is restricted only by interpretation
of each movement concept. In my experience, it is wise to keep
students unaware of the dance outcome (the gusts of wind) or
they may limit their responses to their preconceptions of how,
in this case, the wind might be depicted. Improvisation becomes
restricted as soon as this idea is presented but the already identified action and qualitative content in the above example should
be free of clichéed associations and will be much broader and
perhaps more original than it would have been if the wind
image were to be imparted from the outset.

A development of this improvisation task could lead to exploration of the use of the above concepts in partner relationships
and then further partner movements could be explored and
improvised by one of the pair manipulating the other in movements such as pulling, pushing, wrapping, leaning over/on. A

duo expressing movement of the wind could result from such structured improvisations.

An extension of this work could result in adaptations made to the 'wind' duo in order that selected movements from it are developed and varied for a different but related expressive purpose. In this context, students could be given alternative themes to choose from, such as an argument, parent/child relationship or war. With a number of choices in respect of accompaniment such as poetry, music and sound effects, students will need to improvise various extensions and adaptations of their ready-made motifs in order to find appropriate and original content for their compositions.

This method of guiding improvisation towards a rich and interesting outcome might well serve as an approach in the choreographic process of individual choreographers. In this case, as with the teacher cited above, the composer could lead dancers into improvisations having brainstormed ways in which the theme of 'conflict' might be explored. The method of identifying analogous situations such as the wind or stormy weather will often work well to produce imaginative improvised movement responses which can then be manipulated by the composer.

The above example commences as a tightly limited improvisation task in that each movement concept sets a very restricted boundary. It then opens up to allow the students greater imaginative freedom in responding to the ideas of wind and relationship conflicts respectively. Clearly, the role of improvisation in the exploratory processes of composition is important from start to finish.

IMPROVISATION IN FRAMEWORK COMPOSITIONS

This methodology in dance composition is presented as a teaching device in *The Art of Dance in Education* (1994) but it is also a very appropriate method for composers who wish to employ their dancers as creative contributors to dance works. Indeed some professional choreographers use this method exclusively. The central concept here is reiterated as follows:

a dance framework is a composed structure for a dance denoting what kind of movement [will be featured] in each section, the order of the sections and how these relate to make a whole dance. The [dancers] fill in the detail of the movement content in their own way. ... A well-made ... dance framework has a clear beginning, middle and end, contains variety and contrast, develops logically and achieves coherence of form.

(Smith-Autard, 1994, p. 51)

Here the composer has interpreted the theme and has an imagined dance in his/her head. The dance movements will derive from *framework tasks* given to the dancers and these will provoke improvisation limited to the composer's interpretation of the theme. For example, a duo about changing relationships over time might be structured as follows:

Section 1   meeting and participating in youthful innocent, playfulness;

Section 2   becoming dependent on each other and developing a close loving relationship;

Section 3   in separation by distance growing away from each other in lifestyle, thoughts and feelings;

Section 4   together again but in conflict;

Section 5   resolution – parting or not?

Each of the above sections would be imagined and worked on by the composer so that an *outline* of dance content could be used as framework tasks. This might be achieved on paper or through the composer physically improvising and trying out ideas in order to discern the movement concepts to be presented to the dancers. For the beginning of section 1 for example, the dancers could be led into exploration of travelling actions to meet, hold momentarily and let go in a variety of ways depicting a playful mood. The dancers would improvise within the limitations set and in this way provide the composer with live and moving explorations of the movements to depict the idea. From these improved explorations the composer would select and subsequently set the content for this part of the dance.

The dance framework, therefore, becomes the outer structure within which there are many inner structures (framework tasks). The dancers could be contributors to all or parts of the structures making up the dance. Indeed, they may contribute to the devising process of the overall dance framework as well as to the parts as described above. Here at the outset, when brainstorming and discussing an idea for a dance, improvisation of content can occur in an imagined form. In whatever way the dancers are engaged in the process of composing the dance, improvisation and exploration, either physically or mentally, are the means to the end.

As indicated above, creating a dance framework constitutes setting a range of exploratory improvisation tasks. A teacher of beginner composers could use this method to help the students learn how to improvise within limitations as exemplified above. However, in my view, it is most helpful to all composers to learn the methodology itself. Understanding what a framework composition is can be likened to understanding how to plan an essay or storyboard a film. To identify a structure for the dance overall and the elements within it helps to clarify how students could structure their own improvisation tasks. This activity could be undertaken in collaboration with other student dancers or alone.

A dance framework, then, defines the boundaries for improvisation. How to utilise the improvisation that results from response to a framework task is considered below.

GUIDING IMPROVISATION VISUALLY
This method of structuring improvisation for composition either from 'inside' or 'outside' the piece, is often employed in group choreography.

In the first instance, the dancers might work collectively. This could possibly be categorised as free, spontaneous and unlimited improvisation in that each individual does not know what others are going to do and therefore has to react instantaneously. Like a conversation in movement, limitations are apparent of course, because responses depend upon what is 'said' first and a logical picking up of ideas between dancers will occur. However, as in conversations, there can always be a complete change of topic/idea. Dancers engaged in group improvisation often find new, inspiring departures from their own movement responses when they are forced to do so by the way in which others move. This will not occur, however, if the group is always working together. Hence the wisdom of seeking and adding new people for group improvisation experiences.

Improvisation in a group is generally guided visually by how dancers respond to what they perceive in others' movements.

But just which aspects are picked up on is entirely a responding dancer's decision. It may be the type of action and speed or rhythm of the movement, its pathway and direction or the force and dynamic qualities. One or more of these elements could be replicated, extended and developed in the response or used as a basis for contrast to present an opposing 'point of view'.

Sometimes, however, and especially in contact improvisation contexts, the improvisation is guided not so much visually but by touch or bodily contact between dancers. Here, letting the movement come in the giving and taking of weight, in being manipulated and manipulating others in relaxed but controlled situations in which the lead shifts from one person to another without verbal communication, can lead to some very interesting duo and group movement ideas.

Such improvisations may also be guided and inspired by a composer standing 'outside' the group. Many professional choreographers work this way. Here, the composer has a visual moving canvas which can trigger different directions for the choreography even if it has been pre-designed into a framework composition. Here the composer will have 'set the task' and so the constraints/limitations on the dancers will be defined. The composer viewing the ongoing improvisation can either mentally register what is going on or verbally comment on it. The latter might be in the form of requests to the dancers to repeat or extend the movement ideas or interventions of alternative ideas to push the improvisation forward in different ways.

Whether composing from the 'inside' or 'outside' the dance, the next step, of course, is to recall, select and establish movement ideas for the composition from the improvisation. The dancers may be required to recall come of the most significant moments for them, or the composer will indicate which aspects they should work on. Another way of working is to use video in order to capture the creative moments.

A great advantage in working from the outside is the fact that *relationships* between the dancers can be seen and moments of, for example, complementary, contrasting or overlapping canon in movement, could be identified and refined for the composition.

Guiding improvisation visually, even for a soloist by use of mirrors or a video, can be a very exciting and dynamic event. However, it is very unlikely that composition will emerge unless some ideas have been structured/discussed beforehand. Group improvisation might well be beneficial for its own sake, but when it is used as a means to a composed dance, there should be guidelines to determine the ways in which the outcomes will be used or adapted for the composition or discarded. Framework compositions, discussed earlier, may well prove to be most useful guidelines in this regard.

IMPROVISATION AS PROCESS IN COMPOSITION

Most of the above text has been concerned with improvisation in the context of the preliminary exploratory work or search for starting points which might initiate the process of composition. The diagram at the end of *Methods of Construction 1*, however, indicates that improvisation is likely to have a role throughout the process of composing a dance. Perhaps it is in this context that it is more appropriate to use the term 'exploration' to describe the process of manipulating and adapting the already selected movements to create further material by making developments, variations and/or contrasting passages. The definition of exploration offered at the beginning of this chapter suggests that this is a wholly intellectual process. In my view, this is not the case.

Exploring a range of possible outcomes from a given set of movements requires imaginative, intuitive 'letting go' in improvisation to achieve a richness and originality of outcome. Somehow the composer has to 'get inside' and absorb fully the part of the dance already made and then allow subsequent movements to relate to the original through an intuitive sense of developing form. This is why composers often repeat the first section or the part of the dance already composed in order to produce some new ideas for the next part. A feel for logical progression and relatedness of the new to the old will often emerge through this process.

Exploration through improvisation probably occurs throughout the process of composing. It is the means of driving the composition into new directions and the composer may find moments of insight to produce original progressions in the developing dance.

THE ROLE OF EVALUATION

From the above it is clear that improvisation can be about taking risks, abandoning rules and guidelines to arrive at free and unrestricted responses. Nonetheless, however unrestrained it is, if it is to be used in any way for composition purposes, there is always an element of evaluation taking place. This will lead to decisions to select particular movements from the improvisations which seem appropriate to the idea for the dance and a discarding of those that do not. The selection and adaptation of movements is effected through evaluation of the appropriateness and originality they are judged to have in the context of the composition and original motivations for the dance. In this way, evaluation acts as a moderating, guiding influence on the improvisation, providing a means of achieving an overall holding form.

It is difficult for young and inexperienced composers to find a balance between 'letting go' and 'holding on' to the rules/ guidelines of the discipline of dance composition. The process of evaluation at first requires objective application of knowledge of principles of form, for example, so that understanding of the concepts is developed. Hence, much of the evaluation of improvisation is likely to take place as a class activity where discussion of the relevance of improvised outcomes can lead to knowledge and understanding of the criteria governing emerging forms. To learn how to view and evaluate the improvisation of others is extremely valuable. Here, the teacher can help by reminding students of the task and the idea for the dance on the one hand and compositional principles previously studied on the other. Guiding the viewer's perceptions through questions on worksheets which require written responses might be a way of developing reflective evaluations. But it would probably be necessary to video the improvisation for this activity since beginner students will remember very little from one improvisation. To repeat it physically is self-defeating, of course.

Sometimes, however, the evaluative responses should be verbal and immediate both from the performers and viewers. Little moments of imaginative improvisation may otherwise be lost in the process of too much thinking (especially if they have not been captured on video). Immediate responses are likely to be derived more from feeling the sensations of moving or from viewing the movements of others or oneself with the aid of a mirror; they can often lead to observation and evaluation of fresh and inspired moments.

More experienced composers will probably evaluate the improvisations through informed intuitive responses – sensing or feeling what is right. Whether experienced or not, however, they should not underestimate the importance of evaluating improvisation for the purpose of composition. Hence, the more improvisation experienced and the more professional dance seen, the greater the knowledge gained to inform evaluation. A gradual shift from objectively applied knowledge to a more intuitive guiding of evaluation will take place as experience grows.

CONCLUSION

This chapter has discussed in detail some approaches to improvisation because of its importance in a comprehensive course in dance composition. It is placed here at the end of Section 2 as a corollary because, as made clear above, improvisation as a process towards composition requires evaluation and this is informed through the practice of composition and learning about its underpinning principles and conventions.

Although improvisation can be experienced as a process in its own right, this chapter has, for obvious reasons, placed emphasis on its role in composition. Improvisation, however, has become more significant in late twentieth-century new or experimental dance contexts. Some of these contexts and ways in which improvisation features, are discussed in the following chapter.

Methods of Construction 8
Alternative and Experimental Approaches in Dance Composition

The purpose of this chapter is not to expose the theories or histories behind the various forms of new or post-modern dance. Rather, it concentrates on three defining and distinctive characteristics distilled from study of a range of professional examples and demonstrates how student dance composers can employ some of the variations within them to extend and vary their own composition techniques.

MEANING OF TERMS

Attempts to define the meaning of the terms used to label 'alternative' and 'experimental' approaches in dance composition are fraught with difficulty. In the professional world of dance, these approaches allegedly commenced in the 1960s at the Judson Memorial Church in New York (Jordan, 1992). The label 'post-modern' was used at this time by the dance practitioners themselves, and it has been confirmed by writers such as Sally Banes in *Terpsichore in Sneakers*, first published in 1980 with a second edition in 1987. In Britain, the term 'new dance' has been coined for the experimental practice extending from the early 1960s to the present day. So both labels seem to be appropriate in describing alternative and experimental work which takes different directions in relation to mainstream modern or contemporary dance. There is no single approach and no one set of ideas. Rather, as Mackrell (1992) states in the context of British New Dance:

> It is a revolution which has been partly about choreographic experiment and partly about altering the way people think about dance . . . It is a movement which has been fuelled by political and artistic ideas, all of which have helped to shape the dance scene as we know it today. (p. 1)

Clearly, experimentation is one factor common to the various approaches. However, reflection on reading in this area, numerous viewings and practical engagement in such diversity, lead to a classification and characterisation of such practices under three headings:

- alternative movement contents and eclectic trends,
- different themes and readings of the themes,
- alternative and experimental approaches to dance composition.

The means towards these ends are generally experimental in that exponents consciously break 'rules' of past practices and develop new 'vocabularies', 'rules' or 'methods' which characterise their work. Since these dance makers usually work as individuals, there are as many variations of practice as practitioners. Hence the difficulty of marshalling such idiosyncratic approaches under one label.

ALTERNATIVE MOVEMENT CONTENTS AND ECLECTIC TRENDS

Alternative to what? – might be the first question the reader asks. Throughout this book there has been an underlying assumption that dance composition students should not be restricted in choice of content to one or even two pre-formulated dance techniques such as ballet, Graham or Cunningham. Indeed, Section 1 of this book advised that students should become knowledgeable about an open framework within which they might explore and discover movement content for themselves. The framework proposed was synthesised by Laban having studied natural movement in different contexts. Although the creative approach allied to Laban's principles has been superseded by the 'art of dance' approach (see Smith-Autard, 1994), twenty years on from the first publication, it is maintained that the principles outlined by Laban and summarised on page 19 in this book, are still valid frames of reference for students in creative invention of their own dance contents.

Conversely, learning how to stylise movement content through an understanding of particular techniques such as those of Graham, Hawkins and Humphrey, or ballet, jazz and social dance forms, also constitutes an important part of the discipline of dance composition. Hence the discussion in *Methods of Construction 6*.

Clearly then, both the creative–open framework and technique-based approach, should be experienced in building up a vocabulary of movement for dance content. (This is proposed and discussed further in Smith-Autard, 1994, pp. 17–22).

In both the latter and this book, however, there is emphasis on learning from professional art works and it is through the study of new or post-modern dance exponents of the last thirty or so years, that we see the emergence of a whole range of new dance contents which are gradually replacing or merging with the older, established and conventional techniques. It is this new range of contents emergent from experimental approaches to movement for dance composition that is the focus here.

One of these new vocabularies, becoming increasingly dominant in contemporary dance today, even in more mainstream choreography, is 'Contact Improvisation'. This is supported by Matheson (1992) who claims that:

> Paxton – a former Cunningham dancer, ... was instrumental in the creation of Contact Improvisation in 1972. This duet form, with its roots in a variety of disciplines including wrestling and martial arts has a worldwide network of participants ... Many young choreographers have incorporated the principles, vocabulary and partnering techniques of Contact Improvisation into their dances.
>
> (pp. 217–8)

Contact Improvisation, as the name implies, is improvisation, mostly in duo form (though larger numbers can engage in it when experienced) to create close contact movement 'conversations'. Movements such as leaning on, rolling over, lifting, pushing, pulling, balancing on, wrapping round, tipping or throwing off and catching are employed through physical contact in a variety of relationship contexts. The partners initiate or follow each other's movements; this produces a fluid, ongoing movement improvisation.

The movements can be violent and aggressive or gentle and caring. Whatever the expression, there has to be a relaxed giving into and taking of each other's weight so the focus is inward rather than directed at an audience and the movement is natural rather than extended. Moreover, in moving around, under, through, over, in close, away from each other and fluently going with the momentum, there is likely to be much change of direction and bodily shaping of the pair and very little concern for line or sense of front. Hence the 'rules' governing conventional presentation are not important any more and new principles emerge to guide evaluation of such improvisations.

The originating motivation for this technique – free and spontaneous improvisation of bodily contact movements – has sometimes been superseded by choreographers' use of it in conventional theatre settings in set dance works often accompanied by music or words. This puts new movement content into a more conventional context and removes the element of risk involved in improvisation. It also, perhaps, puts restrictions on performance of the duos in that the dancers, to some extent, will reorientate their movements in alignment to an audience. Nonetheless, in order that the vocabulary is not changed or undermined, the inward focus of the duo has to remain intact. The performers cannot project focus out to the audience whilst engaged in various lifting, rolling, leaning movements – their concentration has to be on and with each other.

Dance composition students have found this technique to be an accessible and almost indispensable vocabulary of movement in expressing some of today's issues – but more on this later. The essential effect of Contact Improvisation has been a freeing up and extending of the ways in which two people can relate in movement terms. We now see a much greater variety of lifts, women lifting women or men and vice versa, of falls and rolls. An eclectic mix of natural movement, martial arts, wrestling and tumbling actions – which inspired Paxton's Contact Improvisation – and an increasing range of content emanating from its use and development by various choreographers, have created an extensive new dance vocabulary for dance composition. Frequently combined with release techniques, the weighted, relaxed feel and look of the movement content provides students with a new domain in which they can experiment to find their own particular ways of using it. The previous chapter presented an example context for such experimentation in that students were set the task of adapting some of the throwing, pulling, pushing, lifting, etc., movements experienced in improvisation based on images of wind to express human conflict. Experimentation with various Contact Improvisation movements would extend the partner relationship possibilities and add richness to the range of movements used in contact.

An alternative shift away from rigid and conventional dance techniques has frequently led choreographers to revert to basic and everyday movement as content for composition. David Gordon was one of the leading exponents in this regard. His dancers of the 1960s had ordinary bodies of all shapes and sizes and moved in very natural everyday ways – walking, running, rolling, lying, sitting, gesturing and stillness. His dance pieces have become more theatrical recently, but they are still recognisable for their pedestrian movement with its 'laid-back sense of casualness where nothing is ever strained' (Robertson and Hutera, 1988). In Gordon's pieces everyday and abstract natural body movements are always highly organised in space, time and group patterning, but they look and feel totally natural, unhampered by technical demands.

Some choreographers have gone to extremes in the use of everyday functional movements such as cooking beefburgers in front of audiences, but in most cases they have applied chore-ographic constraints/rules to make what a lay person would claim as 'even I can do that' into a disciplined and complex outcome beyond the capability of totally untrained dancers. Some of the choreographer devices invented to arrive at such outcomes will be discussed below.

Everyday actions can be used in conjunction with Contact Improvisation and indeed seem to be a logical means of making transitions or moving individually between contact duos, since the same style of weighted, free, relaxed movement without conventional technical demands such as stretched feet, line and uplifted bodies, is apparent in both vocabularies. Students will find such movement easier to manage, but even everyday move-ment needs to be selected, given particular rhythmic and spatial shape and linked carefully into phrases. The choreographic processes will impose such discipline.

Everyday actions especially 'minimalistic' gestures are the basis of vocabulary for several choreographers, most notably, in Britain, Lea Anderson. The Cholmondeleys, her all-female company, often perform small movements of the head and hands, or make imperceptible changes in posture in sitting, lying or standing positions, all of which appear totally natural and easy to do – until they are attempted. Co-ordinating and sequencing movements of various unconnected small body parts into rhythmic and precise sharp movement patterns take time to achieve, especially in unison with other dancers – one of Anderson's characterising features.

Another characteristic evident in some of Anderson's works is the use of a mix of dance genres. As Mackrell (1992) says, Anderson:

> often raids other dance forms for movements and gestures – incorporating ballet, flamenco, ballroom and Scottish folk dance. Sometimes she parodies them . . . but often the movements are integrated into her own style . . .
>
> (Mackrell, 1992, p. 58)

Such eclectic treatment of movement leads to further alternatives in dance movement content. Here, there is frequently a base technique which becomes altered through the incorporation of various elements from another technique. Shobana Jeyasingh, for example, has developed a new vocabulary by injecting some Western contemporary dance elements into what was an essentially purist Bharatha Natyam style. Changing the rhythmic content to fit Western style music, or dancing the original rhythms against melodic continuous sound, makes for subtle differences in nuances of expression in, for example, *Configurations* (1992). Further transformations in movement content are beginning to emerge in her choreography because she is taking more risks in bringing together Bharatha Natyam and contemporary dance techniques. The result of this in *So Many Islands* (1996) is fascinating. The dancers use the floor, extend legs and stretch out arms, glide through level changes into and out of group shapes, yet the Bharatha Natyam style is never sacrificed. Such subtlety of interaction between two seemingly disparate styles produces an exciting new and eclectic vocabulary of dance movement. If students were to experience such movement marriages in practical workshops, they too could learn about different styles and develop their own mixes of them. The influence of South Asian dance (as above), African dance, Street Dance or Rock ''n' Roll styles, for example, changes and extends contemporary dance vocabulary in many varied directions.

Students should explore all the above alternatives in dance movement vocabulary so that they can draw from a range for their own compositions. As indicated above, artists' workshops are a good way of informing them of such vocabularies. Methods of coming to know new and different dance vocabularies are discussed further in the following Section on resource-based teaching/learning of dance composition.

THEMES AND READING OF THEMES

Cunningham, put at the spearhead of post-modernism by Copeland (1983), influenced the removal of expression, representation or the symbolic from much of the experimental choreography of the 1960s and 70s. As Jowitt (1988) states:

> His dancers play no roles, assume no emotions on demand, or pretend to a goal beyond the accomplishment of the dancing (p. 278)

There is no story, no intended meaning, in Cunningham's choreography. If meanings are perceived they are individually created by members of the audience. His dance works feature pure movement and stillness. For example, *Summerspace* (1958) contains simple hops, jumps and turns, rapid travelling runs and long pauses. This puts emphasis on natural bodily actions of the body: 'just dancing' for its own sake. Although his recent works have become more and more technical (for example, *Points in Space*, 1986), the stripping away of expression or symbolic meanings in the movement content has remained a characteristic of his choreography to date and this has been very influential in the work of many other dance makers.

Cunningham bases his movement vocabulary on nature and the natural. He observes the movement of his dancers, people in the street, animals, objects, in order to discover and experiment with the unexpected in terms of gesture, stance and rhythmic movement. His unequivocal interest in chaos influences his treatment of movement as subject in that there is a random interplay and discontinuous illogicality in the juxtaposition of phrases. This signals that 'movement as theme' (for the works) lays particular emphasis on the *manner* of composing which will be discussed later.

Many dance practitioners took this 'movement for its own sake' route in their alternative experimental dance journeys. Trisha Brown, Yvonne Rainer, David Gordon, Lucinda Childs, to name but a few working in the USA, made movement the theme. Rainer, for example, in *Trio A* (1966) constructed movement on the lines of 'minimalist sculpture' (Foster 1986). She goes on to say:

> Throughout its single sustained phrase, made from an eclectic blend of twists, swings, walks, bends, rolls, kicks, lunges, balances, crouches, and smaller gestural movements of the head and arms, no moves were repeated. . . . Instead of shapes and poses or organically developing phrases, *Trio A* offered only transitions, a continuous sequence of actions without pauses or dynamic changes of any kind. . . . Rainer's *Trio A* gave bodily action a sense of accustomed economy.
>
> (p. 174)

Here then, as in others' works, the sheer concentration on movement requires an intellectual response from its audiences:

for example, recognising mathematical patterning in multiple combinations and spatial perspectives in Child's work, and phrases broken up and regrouped in differing spatial and relationship configurations in Brown's pieces. Some British practitioners also fall into this category: notably in her early period, Butcher, who studied and was influenced by the post-modernists in New York.

Moving away from movement as theme to the other extreme of dramatic action, Pina Bausch is claimed as a 'trailblazer' and a 'revolutionary providing the first genuine alternative to the American post-modernists' (Robertson and Hutera, 1988). The highly emotional expressionist pieces (sometimes four hours long) force the audience to identify with the innermost psychological perspectives of individuals and their relationships, especially man/woman relationships. As stated by Robertson and Hutera:

> Her international company of twenty-six performers seem to use the innermost secrets of their lives as the springboard into these performances. They spew out their guts both physically and emotionally with an honesty that has become the byword for all of the Bausch imitators.
>
> (p. 228)

This emphasis on personal realities has produced the label 'theatre of experience' to describe Bausch works. Her motivations may well be confrontational in that she 'reduces the distance and brings "reality of the wishes" into uncomfortable proximity' (Servos and Weigelt, 1984). Bausch intentionally makes the audience cringe in fear, feel desolate and anxious about victimisation – especially of women at the hands of men – and feel disgust in the face of discrimination. By dealing with such psychological, political and social themes, Bausch is concerned to cause a reaction to such realities. She is less concerned with aesthetic appeal and audiences liking her work.

DV8 Physical Theatre has been linked to the work of Pina Bausch. Here too there are no punches pulled. Lloyd Newson's choreography probes issues, for example, gender and sexuality issues and deals with them taking 'daring physical risks which parallel the emotional risks' (Robertson and Hutera, 1988).

Dance students in higher education might also address such themes and emulate the dramatic but non-narrative ways in which they are treated by artists like Bausch and Newson. Following a good deal of experience in viewing and study of the abstract and fragmentary methods used to present these themes, students can be given tasks that collect evidence on a particular issue (racism, for example) and then they can set about making a storyboard out of the seemingly unconnected pieces. This montage effect in the treatment of a theme allows for many different ideas and even personal experiences to enter the dance piece as the group works on it.

A cross-referencing mode of treating themes is also occurring in today's practice in post-modern or new dance contexts. This might occur by means of referencing new dance works with old ones. For example Matthew Bourne's *Nutcracker* and *Swan Lake*, Mats Ek's *Giselle* or cross-referencing with other art forms such as Ian Spink's *De Gas* (1981), which derived from Degas' impressionist paintings, and his *Further and Further into the Night* (1984) which is based upon incidents in Alfred Hitchcock's thriller, *Notorious*. Informed viewings and reading, together with discussion of these choreographers' works, can lead to students attempting to research ways in which they can make cross-references in their work as exemplified with great skill by Spink. Jordan (1992) underlines Spink's treatment of themes in describing how his works:

> mix imagery from a variety of sources and, by revitalising ideas in new contexts, demonstrate the fluid relationship between a sign and its meaning, between signifier and signified. In this respect, they are certainly post-modern ... pieces draw unashamedly from history or the real world of the present, rather than making supposedly 'original' stories: they borrow from politics, personal history, high and vernacular art. (p. 200)

Clearly, the artists mentioned above usually take from the original and alter it so that the cross-reference is presented in such a way as to make the audience think about the original – its political innuendoes, or clichéd meanings. For example, Burnside (1994), in discussing Bourne's *Nutcracker*, suggests that:

Bourne's great skill is to take the visual clichés such as oppressed waifs and deftly exploit their comic potential by twisting them slightly askew. He takes elements of a movement style and sets them to work producing tableaux worthy of a nineteenth-century genre painter and then dissolves them into something else undermining their pathos.

(p. 39)

Hence, the message is often a reinterpretation of the old idea from a modern cultural perspective. The reinterpretation therefore conveys much about contemporary society.

From the above, a mere tip of the iceberg has been revealed in discussion of post-modernists' themes and their treatments of them. Attention has been given to two extremes – composers who deal with movement as theme and composers who take up political and social issues or attempt to deal with psychological behaviours in some way. The tremendous variety between, and at, these extremes cannot be given attention here, but the study of dance composition, specially at university level, should include investigation of these themes and choreographic treatment of them so that the students' own practice is informed and extended.

ALTERNATIVE AND EXPERIMENTAL APPROACHES IN DANCE COMPOSITION

If there is such a person – the grandparent of experimental alternative approaches in dance making – it has to be Cunningham. He had been Graham's leading male dancer, so that in inventing alternative approaches he was directly opposing well-known and established procedures in modern dance choreography. He became leader of the movement away from:

– drama and symbolic dance movements to express plots/feelings,
– using music as an inextricable part of the expressive and rhythmic form,
– hierarchies of role within dance works in which the lead is always in the centre,
– conventional settings and use of performance space,
– conventional structural devices of form (*Methods of Construction 5*),
– expecting emotional responses from audience.

As indicated in the first part of this chapter, some of his movement vocabulary was inspired by observing natural phenomena and so it became simple and pedestrian. However, his dancers have always been technically able and today it is increasingly the case that their technique (the Cunningham technique) is as demanding and stylised as the Graham technique. So, although never celebrated for its own sake, the technique alone is no longer an antithesis to mainstream modern dance; but every other aspect of Cunningham's work certainly fulfils this brief.

Cunningham's concentration on intrinsic features or qualities in movements and/or space and time provides audiences with abstract, kaleidoscopic comings and goings of dancers in the varied performance spaces. There is no intentional expression of meaning to be derived from the pieces nor is the viewer's eye directed at any time. Rather, the placing of dancers all over the space, moving simultaneously in differing ways requires that a viewer makes a choice about where to look and the order in which the images are perused.

A summary of some of the compositional features in post-modern/new dance works, many of which derive from Cunningham, are listed below:

a) alternative use of time which gives it an autonomy in that it is dissociated from the sound and often dancers employ their own patterns in time and speed unrelated to others;

b) alternative use of space by shifting movement incidences to different locations on the stage or performance environment; moving in and facing unconventional directions such as from front to back while facing the back;

c) alternative chance of interrelationships between the number of dancers as solos, duos, trios and so on;

d) alternative ways of juxtaposing and ordering sequences of movement through the use of chance and/or other organisational strategies which result in alternative concepts of form for the dance as an entity;

e) alternative sound co-existing independently with the dance and often changes in the sound used for a piece and alternative co-existence of structures or design elements in the dance space which constitute static or moving parts of the piece but usually having only an arbitrary relationship with the movement content.

For the purposes of discerning ways in which alternative and experimental approaches in dance composition can be tried out by student composers, each of the above listed approaches will be discuss with some reference made to practising choreographers' works. As stated above, it is possible here to refer to only a few of the many choreographers working with alternative approaches. However, constant reference to professional exemplars is a necessary strategy in this sort of work. The importance of resource-based teaching/learning in this context cannot be stressed enough. A range of alternative and experimental work should be 'on tap' to students so that they learn that there are as many different ways of employing each of the above approaches as there are choreographers exemplifying them.

USE OF TIME

a) alternative use of time which gives it an autonomy in that it is dissociated from the sound and often dancers employ their own patterns in time and speed unrelated to others

Cunningham 'let each movement or set of movements "find" its own time'. (Jowitt, 1988) This can be a rewarding and interesting way of playing with the time orchestration of dancers in space. For example, if five dancers perform the same movement sequence each could decide when to perform or hold still, when to move slowly or fast with or without stops, to accelerate, decelerate, move in slow motion, or double time and so on. The result will probably be different in each performance if the time and speed aspects are improvised. The outcome will result in chance unison, canon through overlap, movement against stillness and high energy focus against quiet background, without or independent of, a sound accompaniment.

Another variation in the use of time is discussed in Banes (1980):

> Uninflected phrasing, which Rainer made paradigmatic in *Trio A*, had the effect of flattening the time structure so that dynamics no longer participated in the design of the dance over time. (p. 16)

Students find this challenging in that emphasis removed from dynamics places more importance on the action, space and perhaps relationship aspects of movement. Several exponents in post-modern or new dance employ this use of time in group unison.

USE OF SPACE

b) alternative use of space by shifting movement incidences to different locations on the stage or performance environment; moving in and facing unconventional directions such as from front to back while facing the back

Again, Cunningham has been instrumental in making changes in the use of space in contemporary choreography. In terms of location in the dance space, the centre is no longer emphasised in importance. Sometimes the only extended movement happening is at the back of the space which can only be seen in glimpses through the dancers either standing or moving in front of this. Even Kylian, a mainstream choreographer, employs this use of space (e.g. the final duos section in *Symphonies of Psalms*, 1978). Cunningham and others after him have challenged the conventions in use of locations for particular expressive purposes (see Section 1 in this book and Humphrey (1959), *The Art of Making Dances*). Students can experiment with alternative approaches by placing dancers in unusual locations such as at one side of the space, at the back or even in the audience. A very interesting approach derived from drama is to present the piece 'in promenade' in a large space or in a series of rooms so that the audience has to move in order to see the dance.

Emphasis on the use of different directions is not particularly experimental since all choreographers aim for variety in this respect. However, like David Gordon, some choreographers present numerous repetitions at different angles so that there are multiple views. This is achieved by the bodies changing direction in the space. However, an alternative method of moving in different directions, as seen in some of Lucinda Child's early work, is to keep the body facing one direction but to move in many different directions across and around the floor producing intricate geometric patterns. The sheer repetition of movement to create slight variations in the pattern produces a mesmeric shifting kaleidoscopic effect. The focus on spatial pattern created only by simple and dynamically undifferentiated actions produces what has been labelled minimalist composition. It is a discipline in itself to attempt this process so students might benefit from such an exercise, if only to recognize the difficulty of producing minimalist dance pieces.

INTERRELATIONSHIPS

c) alternative chance interrelationships between the number of dancers as solos, duos, trios and so on

The time and space aspects discussed above can be employed by dancers working as soloists, in duos or larger groups. This often produces a kind of dissonance in that two, three or four seemingly separate dances can be presented simultaneously or, perhaps by chance, in canon. Lea Anderson uses this alternative device, for example, in the video version of *Flesh and Blood* (1989) when two unrelated groups present percussive unison gestural sequences creating a kind of dissonance – two different but not dissimilar tunes going on at the same time. Much experimenting with inter-relationships of distinctive and separate solo or group segments can produce rich, varied and complex dance pieces. Here, students are not attempting to find complementary relationships which coherently make a unified whole. Rather, they are dealing with juxtapositions of fragments and retaining and presenting their differences in simultaneous or successive motion.

FORM

d) alternative ways of juxtaposing and ordering of sequences of movement through the use of chance and/or other organisational strategies which result in alternative concepts of form for the dance as an entity

This has led to dance pieces composed:

- of content in fragments,
- parts/sections not logically connected,
- with much use of repetition without development,
- without concern for unity and with no sense of clear beginning, middle and end,
- with no reference to conventional 'rules' such as the importance of climax, transitions, proportion and balance of the parts in relationship.

Hence these alternative approaches make clear departures from the mainstream approaches to form discussed in *Methods of Construction 4*. Such experiments with form are probably the most practised alternative approaches in dance composition.

There are many ways in which juxtapositioning of movements within a sequence or of sequences themselves can occur, plotting of entrances, exits and journeys between dancers as the 'blue-print', or only constraint, for the dance allows for experimentation of movement content and time aspects in pre-determined orders. Conversely, tossing a coin or using a dice will produce random means of ordering content. A set of six movements organised according to the order of six throws of a dice might well produce a repetition of some moves and an absence of others. For example, one dancer may come up with 5,5,3,1,6,5, and another dancer with 2,4,1,2,6,1. Given four dancers with different combinations of the same movements and performed in varied time and space combinations, the outcome can be very interesting. Hence, pre-planning of the dance elements and the instruction to 'use chance ordering methods' can lead to a pre-learned sequence for each dancer put into unplanned group sequences by combining different numerical orders.

Another system is to mix pre-learned sequences in 'real time'. In Trisha Brown's *Line Up* (1976), for example, instructions are given to named dancers by one dancer sitting in the audience. Spontaneous instructions to reverse, to change sequence, to speed up, etc. lead to improvised form out of set content. Indeed, Brown is renowned for experimenting with different systems to determine order. Her different versions of the piece she called *Accumulations* explore, for instance, around thirty movements accumulated as 1; 1,2; 1,2,3; 1,2,3,4; etc. And deconstruct in similar progressive ways. She has also added to the repetition of such patterns a constant splicing between two different monologues about personal experiences totally unrelated to the movement content.

Another practice frequently found in American post-modernists' work is to bring parts of dances previously constructed into new juxtapositions. Brown's *Line Up* (1976 and 1977), for example, has drawn from six other pieces interspersed with the instruction to 'line up'. 'The continuous forming and reforming of lines causes the dance to hover between order and disorder.' (Programme note in Banes, 1980)

In the more dramatic context of Second Stride's *Lives of the Great Poisoners* (1991), a collaging of fragmentary references to three stories about murderers of differing times and places – Medea, Madame de Brinvilliers and Crippen – are interspersed with references to the work of the inventor of leaded petrol and CFC gases, a contemporary murderer of a different kind (Rubidge, 1991). Such interweaving of thematic fragments is also enriched with an integration of dance, design, music, song and spoken text. Spink has done much to bring together such diversity but his theatre cannot be aligned with others using similar choreographic procedures because the content is so different – biased perhaps towards theatre rather than dance.

The mixing of thematic fragments and different art forms with a much more physical range of dance content is perhaps characteristic of most physical theatre choreographers. Bausch, DV8 and Vandekeybus take these routes but they also often employ physical environments and objects as part of the choreographic process. Nonetheless, the principle of montage seems applicable to this range of choreographers, including Spink. Images are constantly changed and built into a complex web of multi-layered sets of inferences. There are no clear links or logical inter-relationships of the parts. Rather the dance works are made up of different aspects of the theme/s sewn together in a 'patchwork' manner.

After study of some of these choreographers' works, students might well create separate sequences of dance movement to employ within the montage of 'events' to be contained in their interpretations of theme. Some of the above-mentioned random ways of deciding on the order, such as numbering them and using dice might be used to determine a non-linear dance form. The insertion of verbal or sung text and varieties of sound-scapes adds to the interchanging 'dance' as opposed to everyday movement content in order to make a mixture of surrealist and realist fragments for the dance composition. In Bauschian style, for example, students may choose to speak of their own experiences/feelings in some sections and to create abstract dance sequences, perhaps using contact improvisation, in other sections of the piece – each section dealing with a different aspect of the theme. Interspersing realistic spoken sections with symbolic dance sequences is a challenging compositional problem. Experimenting with such alternative approaches when juxtapositioning the fragments can lead university students to produce adventurous and original post-modern dance pieces.

Further restrictions in terms of having no climaxes in the piece, for example, and/or making some parts disproportionately longer than others, and/or exposing transitions as important elements or not having any at all, will help students to break the 'rules' that hitherto may have been stringently applied. Such practices, of course, make further 'rules' for the composers if they are to find success in post-modern choreography.

SOUND AND DESIGN ELEMENTS

e) alternative sound co-existing independently with the dance and changes in the sound used for a piece together with alternative co-existence of structures or design elements in the dance space which constitute static or moving parts of the piece but usually having only arbitrary relationship with the movement content

To some extent this has been discussed above. Suffice it to say that much experimentation with different music or sound accompanying any one dance piece should be encouraged. Similarly, montages of music, noise, silence, text and song can be created to accompany the constant changing of image.

Design of structures to invade the dancer's space and/or movable objects such as chairs, stones or water in containers can also provide bases for much experimental work within the piece. Inclusion of such elements often causes changes to the movement content and if they are movable, their intrinsic qualities add to the overall visual images.

CONCLUSION

The alternative approaches discussed in this chapter are but a few within the lexicon. Students should certainly experience such alternatives, but perhaps not until the traditional/conventional practices have been absorbed. As Fraleigh (1987) says:

> New examples do not replace old ones. We recognise the new in reference to the old according to kind and through some level of community agreement . . . In modern dance *new* has often been mistaken for *better*. But if new were necessarily better, art would be too easy, not worth our attention, and of no lasting value.   (p. 129)

Certainly, there are some alternative approaches within the above text that can be explored by younger or relatively inexperienced learners. However, unless the 'rules' or traditional principles of dance composition are learned first (*Methods of Construction 1–6*), it is not possible to experiment with ways in which they can be broken. A study of some of the exponents of post-modern or new dance will alert dance students to the diversity of alternative approaches.

Throughout this chapter, perhaps more than in other chapters, there has been reference made to professional dance works. It is the interplay of learning from such exemplar resources and of experimenting with them, that creates the composers' knowledge of alternative approaches in dance composition.

Focus on resource-based teaching in the next Section is therefore logical and necessary to promote this integrated methodology.

SECTION 3

Resource-based Teaching/Learning of Dance Composition and New Technologies

RESOURCE-BASED TEACHING/LEARNING

This section aims to demonstrate how important it is to use professional dance works as exemplars in teaching dance composition. In all other arts, students learn from the practice and products of past and present artists. Over the past thirty years, there has been a welcome increase in dance artists' work in education. There is certainly much to be gained by students from this live experience, in addition to the occasionally funded theatre visit. Furthermore, students in university are often privileged to work with lecturers who have themselves had professional experience as choreographers or dancers – or both. In this sector, perhaps more than any other, the teaching/learning of dance composition focuses strongly on the work of artists in the field.

There is also an extensive use of linear video to bring students into contact with professionally choreographed works. Indeed, study of selected works on video constitutes an essential element of most dance examinations in public sector schools and colleges.

The above is a consequence of the shift in dance education summarised in the introduction to this book, and analysed in depth in my book, *The Art of Dance in Education* (A & C Black, 1994). The emerging pedagogy from this shift, with its focus on the dance works of professionals, has been termed by myself and others as *resource-based teaching/learning* in dance. However, as is often the case in practical activities, practice has become established before theories underpinning it have been considered, rehearsed and reported in writing. To date – apart from the book mentioned above, other articles from the same source (see *References*), and a practical guide book by Rolfe and Harlow[1] – there is little background literature to guide producers and/or users of dance resource packs. For the most part, the increasing number of video-based resource materials (i.e. videos plus written materials for teachers) lack conceptual frameworks. A possible exception, through its implicit teaching of a method of analysis by application to Siobhan Davies' *White Man Sleeps,* can be found in Sarah Whatley's writing (1999)[2]. However, even here, there is no overt attempt to provide conceptual bases for teaching and learning of dance composition through analysis of the Davies work.

It is proposed in this Section, that teachers need to become conversant with concepts and principles underlying resource-based teaching/learning before they can make full use of resources to further develop their students' knowledge and/or skills. Obviously, in dance as in other arts, such theory is best exposed and expounded through exemplification drawn from the practice and products of artists – the content of resources. Books can only do this in a cursory way through the written word alone. There are problems too, with resources that include books accompanying linear videos. These rely on users being able to identify elements discussed on the video, with no chance to cross-reference parts of a dance piece, for example, except by tedious searching – mostly without the aid of number or menu reference points. Depth in the use of video resource material is severely lacking in dance education at present.

An answer to this problem has to lie in the use of more advanced technology. In a rapidly changing technology environment, a growing number of formats for dance resources is becoming available. These include CD ROM, a computer based format, and – more appropriately in my view – the digital video formats CD-i and DVD. At the time of writing, the former CD-i multimedia platform is judged the best for dance. This is because it offers touch-button, fast access to any part of the dance piece, and its control buttons can slow, freeze, move frame-by-frame and so on, to deliver quality full-screen and projectable moving images by remote control. DVD can offer

[1] Rolfe L. and Harlow M. (1997) *Let's Look at Dance,* David Fulton Publishers
[2] Roy, Sanjoy (ed) (1999) *White Man Sleeps – Creative Insights,* Dance Books Ltd.

these control mechanisms but it cannot, at present, offer much more. Multimedia authoring of resources in CD-i allows much greater depth in use of full-screen video at real-time speed for teaching/learning dance, in that many additional elements can be added – for example, animated drawings, overlaid text, charts to access analysis or breakdown of dance skills, and progressive tasks for students. Appropriate and innovative application of multimedia exposes the intricacies of dance choreography. In addition, such a comprehensive multimedia resource provides a flexible range of material for several contexts – school, university, initial and in-service teacher training – and can be used for both class teaching and student-based distance learning.

A recent publication, *Wild Child – An Interactive CD Resource Pack for Dance Education* (1999)[3], is currently the only example of this much needed type of resource. This pack is also unique in its identification of conceptual bases for the proposed uses of the professional work in dance education. In other words, the pack proposes a rationale and methodology for in-depth teaching/learning of dance composition, performance and appreciation through use of a professional dance work as a resource. The visual dance exemplification presented on CD as digital video is accompanied by text, both on disc and in the *Resource Book,* to explain the theory behind the tasks set for students and the methods that could be applied in the use of the resource to inform and extend practice.

For the purposes of this Section, the above-mentioned resource pack is discussed and analysed to demonstrate how teachers and students of dance composition could derive great benefit from the use of such multimedia resources. As stated above, however, at the time of writing this edition of *Dance Composition,* the *Wild Child* pack is the only multimedia resource of its type in the world. No doubt, there will be others published in the near future[4]. Nonetheless, there is much catching up to do if dance education is to become resourced to make it in any way comparable with music, drama, literature and the visual arts in provid-

---

[3] Bedford Interactive Productions (1999) *Wild Child – An Interactive CD-i Resource Pack for Dance Education,* in collaboration with the Ludus Dance Company. See the *Resource* list at the back of the book for further details.
[4] Bedford Interactive Productions has further titles in preparation. See the back of the book for contact information.

ing access to professional examples of creative work. Technology now offers great opportunities to dance education.

Prior to discussion of the *Wild Child* pack, it is important to confirm what is meant by the term, 'resource-based teaching/ learning'. As part of the pack, the *Resource Book* presents an analysis of the concept[5]:

> The word resource means:
> * something that can be used for support or help
> * an available supply that can be drawn upon when needed[6].
>
> The word source – a main part of resource – means:
> * the thing from which something originates – the starting point
> * something that supplies information that can be used to develop something else[7].

The first usage demands that a resource act as a bank of information that can be used as an advanced teaching/learning aid, or as a means of reference to support work not directly connected with the resource itself. The second usage demands that the resource provide source material for dance work in a variety of contexts.

The resource-based teaching methodology, from the students' point of view, requires that resources be available for their self- or group-directed study purposes. This implies that, for example, given a task to identify, list and comment on the dance content and methods of abstraction employed in a snippet of choreography, the students have access to the snippet plus methods of working. Interactive CD provides an ideal medium for this kind of work, especially through its capacity to freeze-frame, advance frame-by-frame, and return to the start of a selected part of a work by the click of a button. Moreover, if the students have been informed through use of a CD resource pack that teaches the theory behind the practice, they will have understood – through visual demonstration coupled with access to focused

---

[5] Some of the text in this Section was first published in the *Resource Book* – written by Smith-Autard as part of the *Wild Child CD-i Resource Pack* published by Bedford Interactive Productions (1999).
[6] Reader's Digest Universal Dictionary (1987)
[7] Ditto

worksheets – how to apply the appropriate principles of analysis to any dance work.

The pack that is under scrutiny here contains two interactive CD discs, an audio CD disc and a book. The latter is a resource book, not just a manual. The interactive CD discs and the book have been created to augment and complement each other. Obviously, there are aspects of dance that are best studied in visual, full screen, real-time movie form. There are other aspects that can be communicated through 'stills'. In relation to knowledge about dance and how to analyse, study it or teach it, a good deal of information can be clearly presented in the written form. However, as intimated above, there is much more to be gained from a textual explanation of a concept if it is accompanied by examples of moving dance images, than if it were to stand alone.

Hence, for instance, the text in the *Wild Child Resource Book* is able to fully exemplify principles of dance composition through analysis of an actual dance work viewed on screen. So, in this case, readers do not have to translate and imagine, let us say, a particular development of a motif; they have it there moving on screen to aid immediate understanding. It could be claimed, therefore, that the interactive CD discs plus all the writings in the *Wild Child Resource Book* exemplify many of the concepts and principles discussed in the previous sections of this book, *Dance Composition.*

Moreover, the use of both interactive CD discs and the text in the *Resource Book*, fully exemplifies the resource-based teaching/ learning methodology that is currently defined as a model of good practice for all dance teachers and arts teachers generally.

– Wild Child – A CD Resource Pack –

The Ludus Dance Company's production of *Wild Child* – made into an interactive CD resource pack, published by Bedford Interactive Productions – is an excellent visual exemplification of dance concepts for dance education at all levels.

This resource pack is unique, in that it demonstrates a new resource-based teaching/learning pedagogy which can be applied to other resources. The *Wild Child* pack has a huge range of teaching materials. Through many worksheet activities, it teaches *principles, concepts* and *methods* of working in dance composition, performance and appreciation. It therefore has an extensive shelf life and adds to, extends and enhances the use of other resource packs and dance texts.

Unlike many CD ROM discs, the *Wild Child* discs are not dense with text. There are three main reasons for this. First, because there is very little room for readable text on screen alongside reasonably sized movies. Second, because multimedia technology is wasted if it merely replaces paper. Third, and most important, because the book is designed to work in conjunction with – and to reinforce, extend, and supplement – the information contained on the interactive CD discs.

Hence, the open book can be glanced at while studying dynamic, full-screen moving images. Quick reference to the book can also be made while simply pausing the images on screen, rather than going to another level within the disc. It is important to stress therefore, that this availability of the supporting written materials makes for coherent and uninterrupted access to any topic of study.

Additionally, of course, the CDs are *interactive*; this in itself implies constant user interaction with the resource. Moreover, since it is a *resource* – not a self-contained, programmed learning pack – interaction requires that the *user* make the decision on which aspects to employ, and how to use them as a means of furthering or supplementing the dance work in hand. As a resource and a source for a variety of dance purposes, each aspect of the visual material can be employed in different ways. It is the book itself that suggests variable usage of the CDs according to perceived differing needs. A full range of such different approaches is best presented on paper so that work for specific groups of users is contained in separate sections.

The content of the pack is summarised below.

CD RESOURCE DISC 1 – full performance by the Ludus Dance Company of Wild Child*, with choreography by Jane Scott Barrett, and music and artistic direction by James Mackie on full-screen digital video*

a) *Film view* of 56-minute video –*Wild Child*. The dance piece depicts the plight of a 19th century child, abandoned in the forest at a young age. The child is captured as an adolescent and 'civilised' through socialisation into play, love, work and attendance at social events.

b) *Access and Control* screen to provide access to six main scenes and 31 sub-sections of *Wild Child*. The digital video has controls to single shot, stop/go, go back, slow motion and exit.

c) *Viewing and Doing* study linked to the *Resource Book*. This study of the whole work is presented under the following headings:
* Themes
* Dance Content
* Dance Form
* Music and Sound
* Costumes and Set

CD RESOURCE DISC 2 – creative dancework: excerpts of Wild Child *on full-screen digital video*

a) *Composition* includes further study of:
* *Dance Content* – contact/partner work;
* *Dance Form* – detailed analysis through macro and micro analysis charts;
* *Orchestration* – analysis of dancers in time and space.

b) *Performance* study includes:
* *Technique* – contact work, beginnings to advanced sequences;
* *Repertoire* – teaching of two items from *Wild Child*;
* *Performance Qualities* – study or practice of artistic qualities to improve performance.

c) *Appreciation* study includes:
* *Aesthetic Qualities* – perception of sensory, expressive and formal qualities.

RESOURCE BOOK

As mentioned above, a distinctive feature of this resource is the strong interrelationship between the CD discs, the book, the teacher and the students while working interactively. To this end, the *Resource Book* is inextricably linked to the content of the discs. Furthermore, *the approach used emphasises the need for responses to questions or tasks, based upon the use of* Wild Child *as a resource and source for teaching and learning in dance performance, composition and appreciation.*

* *Section 1* describes the *Wild Child* resource pack and interactive CD as a medium.

* *Section 2* describes resource-based teaching and learning, and provides more than 80 worksheets to advance dance knowledge and practical expertise in performance and composition. These worksheets are based on the contents of both CD discs.
* *Section 3A* explores the use of the *Wild Child* resource pack for primary teachers, through increasing their own knowledge of dance and their understanding of how to teach it.
* *Section 3B* explores use of the *Wild Child* resource pack for non-specialist secondary teachers, through increasing their own knowledge of dance and their understanding of how to teach it.
* *Section 3C* explores use of the *Wild Child* resource pack for secondary (specialist teachers) and in tertiary dance education.

THE WILD CHILD *PACK AND TEACHING/LEARNING DANCE COMPOSITION*

The pack will have an important impact on students' learning in dance composition, by:

* developing their abilities to perceive, describe, analyse, interpret and evaluate dance work;
* increasing their vocabulary in describing dance and their understanding of terminology;
* demonstrating how themes can be translated into creative ideas for dances, and exploring the themes used in *Wild Child* within their own work;
* increasing their understanding of the processes involved in selecting movement, and in using music, props, set and costumes – thereby extending their abilities to create motifs and build dances;
* introducing, extending and consolidating concepts relating to form in dance composition by means of analysis and appreciation of the choreographic devices used in *Wild Child*;
* making them aware of qualities in the dancers' performance and its effects on the composition;
* encouraging greater autonomy through response to worksheet tasks or student-based activities using the interactive CDs.

To reiterate: it should be clear from the above that this resource pack, unlike any other dance pack to date, develops students' knowledge of *concepts* and *principles* underlying composition, as well as of some of the *methods* used by contemporary chore-ographers.

SOME EXAMPLE USES OF THE WILD CHILD *PACK IN PRACTICAL DANCE COMPOSITION TEACHING*

The *Viewing and Doing* mode of CD Disc 1 contains 50 work-sheets featuring many practical tasks, questions and discussion topics. These worksheets require students to actively use the knowledge gained from study of the various elements contained in *Wild Child*: *Themes, Dance Content, Dance Form, Music and Sound, Costumes and Set*. The worksheet tasks aim to develop the users' skills, knowledge and understanding of dance composition. All the worksheets demand a constant interactive use of the CD discs. Hence, the title – *Viewing and Doing.*

DANCE CONTENT FOR COMPOSITION

In teaching dance composition, the discs make visual some of the highly complex and abstract principles of symbolic content and form which need to be considered by students in creating successful dances. In study of the dance content, beginner students of, say, 14 plus can be guided to perceive and note the range of content used to depict a theme. This is achieved by reference to a chart such as that on the following page, while at the same time viewing the performance on disc.

CONCEPTUAL FRAMEWORK/TOOL – *LABAN'S ANALYSIS OF MOVEMENT*

As indicated earlier in this book, Laban's analysis is the most comprehensive and appropriate analytical tool for dance appre-ciation and composition. This is because it breaks movement down into general principles and concepts which can be applied to any dance style or technique. It is a means by which anyone with knowledge of Laban's principles can observe, describe and analyse movement in detail.

The study of dance content requires that students learn to use Laban's analysis through observing, naming and categorising the emphasised dance content in all the scenes in *Wild Child*. In the *Viewing and Doing* mode on Disc 1, an example of the chart overleaf demonstrates how use of the four main headings – actions, qualities, spatial features and relationships – guides students' perception.

Dance Content Chart for 'School – A PE Lesson'

ACTIONS	QUALITIES
Arms held away from body, fists clenched	Sharp
Steps in directional patterns	Strong
Astride and together jumps	Precise
Pivot half-turns	Accented
Lunges from a fixed base	Energetic
Runs on spot with opposition arms	Rhythmic
Turning jump	Aggressive
Roll	
Run	
Squat into wide stretch	
SPATIAL FEATURES	**RELATIONSHIPS**
Large moves	Use of document on back wall
Constant changes of direction through half and quarter turns	Unison
Square patterning	Three dancers together all the time
Pattern repeated in different places in space	Wild Child separated then joins in
High and medium levels emphasised	Square group shape unchanged

The intention here is to provide students with a conceptual framework, in order that they can turn their attention to particular elements – such as qualities of speed and force – and observe the expressive and rhythmic differentiations created through combinations of these two elements. Students who can perceive detail in content are bound to appreciate the dance in more depth. Moreover, identification of new and interesting movement content will enlarge the students' own vocabulary for composition purposes.

The method of doing this, however, needs to be student-focused so that they find for themselves words to describe the four elements of actions, qualities, spatial and relationship features. To this end, a blank proforma is presented in the *Resource Book* for the teacher to photocopy. The teacher, through questions, could ask students to fill in the details under each heading during several viewings of the piece under scrutiny. Through this activity, students are not only learning about the content of the choreography studied, they are also gaining knowledge of and using a very appropriate tool – Laban's analysis.

A much greater depth of knowledge will derive from the students' practical engagement with the same range of dance content observed on the CD. In respect of the above example, the teacher could select tasks from the worksheet on page 122. These could then be referenced by viewing the dance on disc, to guide the students' practical exploration and use of such content for composition on the theme.

Clearly, use of this worksheet directs students' perception of content, and how this expresses themes in the dance works they view. It also adds vocabulary of movement and methods of selecting, abstracting and refining content for the motifs they create in their own dance compositions. CD Disc 1 provides access to the whole of the work, *Wild Child*. Study of *Dance Content* in the above way is undertaken through the use of 13 charts of content and related practical worksheets.

The work derived from study of the *Themes* and *Dance Content* of *Wild Child* therefore clearly relates to *Section 1 – The Material Content* and *Section 2 – Methods of Construction 1* of this book.

Disc 2 – *Creative Dancework* – offers further opportunities to study *Dance Content* in relation to the *Theme*. Here, there is a focus on contact improvisation vocabulary as used in other sections of *Wild Child*. Several examples of the relationships of initiating, supporting and lifting can be studied and then used as inspirational references to guide the students' own responses to the worksheet on page 123.

Even without knowledge of *Wild Child*, it should be evident to the reader that the use of such a worksheet – in conjunction with interactive study of the video excerpts on the discs – requires students to consider and categorise different types of contact movements. They then further their understanding of these concepts by producing their own versions of each

COMPOSITION

DANCE CONTENT

RELATED PRACTICAL TASKS WORKSHEET
for 'School – A PE Lesson'

Composition and appreciation – creating motifs

1) Watch the first motif in *Step Dance* and list the references to PE or Sport in the movements. Such references are called abstractions[8]. Select six differing sports pictures from newspapers and abstract an action from each. Link these actions into a phrase. For example, a tennis serve may be followed by a cricket or golf drive, and a kick in football could be followed by a thrust in fencing.

2) Imagine and physically rehearse movements used in sport activities – basketball, hockey, tennis, volley ball, canoeing, climbing, track running, athletic throwing events, etc. Select one moment from eight different activities and link these together into a phrase. This process of abstraction and the combination of such abstractions into phrases creates a symbolic representation of 'sport'.

3) Work on altering the rhythm by changes of speed from slow motion to fast. Also, change levels, directions and size of the actions.

4) Develop the actions by adding gestures, jumps, turns and travel between them. Using track 5 of the music, finalise the order, rhythm and phrasing of the movements in an eight-bar motif.

5) Show this work to a partner. He or she should recognise abstractions, commenting on logical progression from one action to the next to achieve continuity and on the rhythm and variety in the motif.

---

[8] Abstraction refers to 'the process of separating inherent qualities or properties from the actual physical object or concept to which they belong' (Reader's Digest *Universal Dictionary*, 1994). The extraction of an essential and recognisable element from an original source is the starting point. The choreographer then needs to alter and add features to it to make it dance. However, the original should always remain recognisable.

COMPOSITION   **DANCE CONTENT**

PRACTICAL WORKSHEET – Love Duo – initiating, supporting and lifting contacts

Appreciation leading to exploration and composition

1) Study the five examples of initiating and supporting actions on the disc to categorise them into initiating or supporting contact movements, or both.

2) With a partner, perform each of the five contact actions to identify its defining characteristics. (For example, the head-in-hand support is very lightly supportive of a body part in contact with the supporter's body part.) Write a list of the defining characteristics.

3) Take each of these defining characteristics and explore them to find at least three other ways of performing such initiating/supporting contact actions.

4) Concentrate on the rhythmic content of each of your contact actions, identifying the use of impulse, impact and swing to create momentum.

5) Link and mix these together to create phrase motifs symbolising a soft, caring relationship.

6) Watch the sub-section *Contact Duo* in the *Love Duo* on Disc 1, to note how extensively the couple travels. Try to use as much floor space as possible while you perform your contact actions travelling from place to place.

7) Work with another couple to share and learn each other's contact phrases.

8) Compose a short dance sequence integrating the two sets of phrases appropriately. The sequence could be based on one of the following ideas:

       trust   dependency   before we part

9) Perform and evaluate the dance, commenting on the effectiveness of the contact actions to express the theme. Also comment on the originality of your contact action material.

category. An additional concentration on the rhythmic pattern of each action, and the ways that they can be combined into phrases to create expression, provides much in-depth learning about dance composition derived from study of the dance work.

There are several other ways of studying contact relationships in *Wild Child* and of using the dance work as a basis for the students' own creative composition work. In each case the *concepts* and *principles* underlying this vocabulary are developed and then utilised in composition tasks.

DANCE FORM FOR COMPOSITION

The 'School' section provides an example of the way in which *Wild Child* can be used to support the teaching of dance form. Although the text in *Methods of Construction 2–5* of this book has been used for the past 24 years, it must be evident to all teachers that it is very difficult to teach the concepts of form without visual exemplification. These concepts are abstract, and again need to be understood as *principles* that can be applied in hundreds of different ways rather than as textbook rules to be learned. Now, for the first time, the form of a dance piece can be studied on screen so that students can see for themselves what is meant by the terms used in this book and how these devices might be employed to structure their own dance compositions.

The disc clearly describes the purpose of this work – to develop appreciation of the form in the choreography through identification of the following choreographic devices:

* Motif
* Section
* Transition
* Repetition
* Development
* Variation
* Contrast
* Climax
* Unity

FORM TIME CHART for 'School' – A PE Lesson

Sections
Step Dance & Learning

A1	A2	B1	A3	B2	A4	A5	B3
Motif	Rep.	Tra.	Rep.	Tra.	Dev.	Rep.	Tra.
8 bars	8	4	8	4	8	4	8

Joins Step Dance

A6	B	A7	A8	A9	B5
Rep.	4	Dev.	Dev.	Rep.	Tra.
8	2	6	8	4	4

Change of Game

C1	C2	C3	B6
Mot.	Dev.	Dev.	Tra.
Con.			
6	8	8	6

Repeats to trial

A10	A11	A12
Var.	Rep.	Rep.
Cli.	Var. Cli.	Var.
6	8	4

In addition, this scene uses patterning in space as an aspect of form. This is clearly seen in the diagrams on the disc (below) that require study in order fully to answer the related questions that follow.

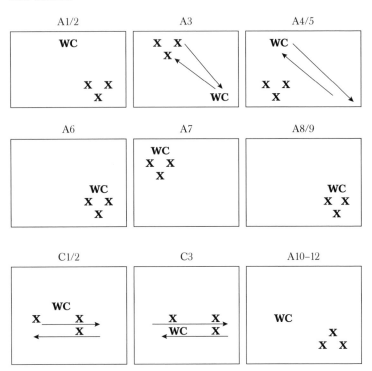

DANCE FORM – RELATED DANCE TASKS
WORKSHEET for 'School'

Appreciation – group discussion or individual tasks to develop perception of form

1) Look at Motif A and describe how the repeats maintain interest though the movements stay the same. Also, look at how the motif is developed in A7 and A8.

2) What makes A10-12 variations rather than developments?

3) Why do you think there are as many repetitions of Motif A in *School*?

4) Look at all the transition elements labelled B. Identify the functions that they have and the similarities and differences between them. Do you agree that they are correctly labelled as transitions?

5) How far do you agree that A10 and A11 constitute the climax of the piece? If you do not agree, give an opinion as to where the climax or climaxes might be.

6) Describe how the interrelationship between the sections labelled A, B and C creates unity of form.

7) To what extent does the form of *School* – including the floor and group patterning – contribute to the theme of this scene in *Wild Child*?

8) Consider the structure of the Wild Child's dance in relation to that of the other three dancers, and discuss how this helps to show him as the outsider and new learner. What happens immediately before and immediately after *School*, and how does this aspect of form consolidate the theme?

Composition

Using material created through the processes of abstraction as required in the study of *Dance Content*, employ the same form/structure and spatial patterning to create a dance based upon learning in a sports context.

Diagrams to represent the form or structure of sections of *Wild Child* are presented. Except in one example case described below, these are not phrase-by-phrase, detailed accounts of the structure. Rather, students are given an overall view of the inter-relations between motifs, repetitions, developments/variations, contrasts, the climax or climaxes, and a picture of the unity achieved through such interrelationships.

Study of the form of the dance piece with reference to the chart below will be greatly enhanced by answering the tasks on the related worksheet that follows. The following chart on the CD allows access to each line/section and to each cell/phrase separately in any order. This means that students wishing to answer question 2, for example, can make immediate reference to A1 then A10, A11, A12 and A7 for comparison to help them answer the question.

MICRO-ANALYSIS OF FORM

A more detailed study of a short part of the 'Play' scene in *Wild Child* can be accessed on CD Disc 2. This micro-analysis demonstrates how motifs, developments and variations – and the successive and simultaneous multilayering of these choreographic devices – produces copying, complementing and contrasting relationships between the four dancers. This is an excellent illustration of the concepts discussed in *Methods of Construction 3* in this book. If students were to study these aspects of form through the use of the *Wild Child* pack, they would be able to apply the concepts to analysis of other works. At the same time, they could feed a more in-depth understanding of such devices appropriate for group compositions in structuring their own dance pieces.

There are several multimedia devices offered to aid analysis – both of the foundational motifs (performed by the Wild Child in this instance), and of the way that this dancer's movements are complemented by means of developments or contrasted by means of variations by the other dancers. It is even possible to follow what each dancer is doing in relation to the Wild Child, through selection of on-screen colour charts that can be viewed at the same time as the full screen video. This very detailed analysis of the intricate layering of motifs, developments and variations for four dancers helps students to perceive and appreciate the complexity and interest that can be achieved through the use of such composition devices. Here again, worksheet tasks will extend their own composition. There are four worksheets in the *Resource Book* to guide in-depth study of the micro-analysis of the form of this part of the dance work. A fifth worksheet encourages students to create their own dances using a similar structure but on a different theme. Hence, having used this part of the resource, students are better able to compose well-structured group dances – having seen how a number of dancers' motifs, developments and variations can occur simultaneously and in succession, to create interesting and unified time 'pictures' for viewers.

MUSIC ACCOMPANIMENT FOR COMPOSITION

A further unique aspect of the *Wild Child* resource pack lies in the facility offered for the study of the musical accompaniment. Disc 1 can be used interactively to:

* hear the music only;
* hear the music and see the dance at the same time;
* freeze the video and listen to the next piece of music, then unfreeze it to catch up with the music accompaniment again.

The technology therefore permits concentration on the music with access to the visual dance performance at the touch of a button. This ensures that students can respond to questions and tasks such as the following, thereby developing their knowledge of music and ways in which it might be used in composition. The following worksheet refers to the same section of *Wild Child* selected for illustration of the study of dance content and form above.

Clearly, the depth of study of the elements in the music and how they relate to the dance piece will inform the students' own use of music in their compositions. There is a great variety of music in *Wild Child*, so this kind of study and use of the music CD for students' own work will also teach them more about music – a necessary but often neglected part of dance education.

MUSIC APPRECIATION WORKSHEET for 'School'

Questions or group discussion topics – to guide the development of appreciation of the music and sound, and how it complements and supports the choreography

1) The sound of children's voices at the start obviously sets the context, but the movement of the pupils on entering for the PE lesson creates a contrast to this sound track. What is this contrast and what effect does it have?

2) Describe how the beat, time signature and rhythm of the music complements the movement and the idea it expresses.

3) How does the music reflect the 'square' sort of quality in the movement and spatial patterning of this section?

4) Repetition of the musical pattern matches the repetition of the movement. How does the music repetition retain interest in the first part of the dance up to the voice-over?

5) Discuss the ways in which the music develops in the whole of the second repetition of Motif A, between the voice-over above and the change of game.

6) Does the music from the change of game to the end of the dance repeat exactly the beginning of the dance? If not, say how it varies.

7) The spoken elements at the end of 'School' are punctuated with movements. What does this add to the sound and what effect emerges from the combination of voice and sound?

8) Describe the overall qualities of the music in 'School' and how they relate to the theme.

COSTUMES, PROPS AND SET FOR COMPOSITION

Similarly, in the context of a section in which the Wild Child is learning about the work place – where there is emphasis on acquisition of wealth (money in a golden egg), and people are concerned to get to the top by fair or foul means (through surreptitious use of ladders) – study of the role of costumes, props and uses of the set in the composition is advanced by responding to questions such as those given in the following worksheet.

Having considered the use of these elements of composition in the 'Work' scene, the students could undertake tasks such as the following exploration of content including use of props, with a better understanding of the ways that props create interest.

COSTUME AND SET   **SCENE: WORK**

APPRECIATION WORKSHEET 2

Questions or group discussion topics – to guide the development of appreciation of the costumes, set and props, and how they complement and support the choreography

Ladders

1) In what ways is the large egg, high up and at the back of the stage, made the main focus in the dancers' movements at the beginning of this section?

2) Using words or phrases such as 'blocking' or 'climbing up', list ways in which the ladders are used as props. Relate these to the theme of work and ambition to get to the top prize.

3) Evaluate the role of the costumes, set and props in depicting the theme and in providing visual interest.

In a group of four, discuss the kind of movements you would use to convey the idea that although you all know where a coveted object is, you each want to find it for yourselves without the others seeing. Also, that you would need to use a chair to stand on to reach it. Work out travelling into and out of the space, and the use of one chair between the four of you to convey this idea (as in *Wild Child*). The chair could be left in the space, moved from place to place, taken out of and brought back into the space. In other words, choreograph the spatial and relationship features for four dancers and the chair using the first section of track 9.

In pairs, both with chairs, work out a sequence to include unison, canon, doing the same and contrasting movement while you relate to the chairs and swap them many times. To add variety, the chairs could be placed in different positions – upside down, on their sides, on top of each other, facing, back to back, etc. Include as many of the actions, qualities and relationship features listed for the 'Ladders' section of *Wild Child* as possible.

ORCHESTRATION OF DANCERS IN TIME AND SPACE

CD Disc 2 – *Creative Dancework* – extends and enhances the study of composition by developing an appreciation of the *orchestration of dancers in time and space*. As discussed in *Methods of Construction 3* earlier in this book, in the context of group dances, much visual interest can be gained by ensuring that the composition includes a richness of changes in *Timing, Numerical* and *Spatial* relationships. This aspect of study on the CD aims to demonstrate the orchestration of dancers in *Wild Child* to inform students' own creative dancework.

Further purposes are:

*   to offer students the opportunity to employ the orchestration of dancers in space and time, as extracted from excerpts of *Wild Child* as *scores* for their own creative dancework;
*   to provide students with some tools for analysis of orchestration, so that they can apply them to other dance works – thereby increasing their knowledge of the multitude of ways in which a group dance can be orchestrated.

As an example, a part of *Wild Child* is presented on the CD as a series of plans. These interleave dance phrases to indicate the main changes in spatial relationship of the dancers on the stage. They also indicate the numerical division of the visible dancers by noting their proximity to each other, as well as group shapes created by the dancers in space.

Variety in *Spatial Relationship, Numerical Division* and *Group Shape* are just *three* elements in a complexity of orchestration. Further elements include:

*   *Timing* of dancers' movements in relation to each other and to the accompaniment.
*   *Floor Patterns* created by the dancers singly and in interaction.

All of these elements, visually exemplified, can be explored further through use of the worksheets in the *Resource Book*. A brief illustration of this makes reference to the plans of dancers' positioning and group shapes in the 'School' scene (*see* page 126 above).

RELATED DANCE TASKS WORKSHEET
for 'Orchestration' (continued)

'School' out of the *Play and School* scene:

1) View the 'School' excerpt using the *Plans* in Section 2:B:3 in the *Resource Book* to follow the outline sketch of the orchestration.

2) Now draw your own plans of this excerpt, filling in any gaps and providing a key to identify the dancers' changes of positions in relation to each other.

3) Now use your own plans as a score for a dance sequence based on one of the following ideas:

* a stranger in our midst;
* a leader emerging.

This work clearly helps students to perceive spatial/temporal/ relationship elements in a dance piece. It is not easy to see such changes in fast moving dance. Nor is it easy to transpose a two-dimensional view into a three-dimensional phenomenon. However, through application of technology to expose the density of orchestration in just one piece as an example, doors are opened to such perception. Moreover, use of digital video controls – slow-motion, frame advance and loop-back – to track such changes allows the students themselves to create 'orchestration storyboards' for any of the other sections of *Wild Child*. Hence again, as required in the above worksheet, principles of orchestration in time and space can be discerned and applied in the students' own compositions.

FURTHER SECTIONS OF THE CD DISCS RELATING TO COMPOSITION

Experienced teachers know that practical work in dance composition is greatly enhanced by the development of dance vocabulary – through technique practice, and through learning and performing pieces of repertoire choreographed by professionals. Furthermore, analysis of dance performance to improve phrasing, variation in qualities/dynamics, focus, alignment, expressive intention and so on, will inevitably inform the students' own compositions. CD Disc 2 contains much useful content under these headings. For example, in the *Repertoire* section, students can learn and perfect excerpts of *Wild Child*, thereby experiencing 'from the inside' the content, form and expressive qualities of the piece. In this way, they learn about the craft from master artists – the choreographer in this instance. Every aspect of work in the *Wild Child* resource pack will therefore directly or indirectly extend and enhance teaching and learning of dance composition.

CONCLUSIONS

However important the content of the *Wild Child* pack might be in delivering multiple visual exemplifications of most of the theory in this book, the fact that it utilises a technology beyond linear video, also appropriately extends the resource-based teaching methodology into the next millennium.

This implies that the rationale for discussion of the multimedia resource featured in this Section is two-fold. First, it has offered readers a chance to imagine (for this is all that can be done without sight of it) how technology can advance practice in the teaching of dance composition referenced by professional dance works. Second, it demonstrates how comprehensive and inventive applications of multimedia can expose the intricacies of choreography for study purposes. Through an embedded, resource-based teaching/learning methodology, students are guided to discover these intricacies and learn from them to extend their own dance composition.

Dance education obviously needs many such visual resources. It is essential that professional companies and artists focus on new technologies to develop multimedia resources for future teaching. Certainly, the teaching of dance composition should become transformed in the next decade or so if this happens.

A further means of technology-aided teaching – through structured design, learning and participation – lies in use of the Internet. As an example, *Hands-On Dance Project* by Popat[9] uses carefully planned frameworks to engage interested participants

[9] Sita Popat has created a Web-site http://goehr.leeds.ac.uk/sita/hands-on/ (1999 and ongoing) to explore the potential of the Internet in dance composition. She is undertaking this as part of a PhD at Bretton Hall, University of Leeds, UK

in an interactive dance-making process. This Web-site is the most advanced of its kind, so it must be taken account of in the context of serious application of technology in teaching/ learning dance composition.

SECTION 4

Standing Back from the Process
The Composer's Freedom

The process of composing a dance varies with each person who attempts it, and no-one can set out rules or methods of progression which can be followed in order to achieve guaranteed success.

When the composer is at work there is constant influence exerted from the inter-relationship of his/her:

1) imagination and intuition,
2) knowledge of movement material,
3) knowledge of methods of construction, and
4) acquaintance knowledge of form, style and meaning in the aesthetic realm which has been gained through experience of seeing other people's dances and art works in forms other than dance.

Until now, this book has been concerned mainly with the areas 2 and 3 above and to some extent 4 has been discussed in the section on resource-based teaching. To consider the inter-relationship further it becomes necessary to attempt more detailed discussion of 1 and 4.

IMAGINATION AND INTUITION
The fact that the composer's imagination and intuition are active during the creation of a dance cannot be disputed. These are elusive qualities and to discuss when they function, and even what they are, is very difficult indeed. The following ideas on some possible roles that imagination and intuition might play in the composition of a dance, are based upon the experience of making dances and discussion with many students both during and after the process of composing.

IMAGINATION

Clearly the dance composer cannot function without using imagination. One of the definitions offered in Webster's Dictionary (1966) is:

> . . . the ability or gift of forming conscious ideas or mental images especially for the purpose of artistic or intellectual creation.

A composer has complete freedom of imagination until he/she has decided on the idea for a dance. Sometimes, this can be a difficult decision if the imagination is fired by many alternative ideas. In choosing a theme, the inexperienced composer is often unaware of the pitfalls when he/she tries – unsuccessfully – to translate great epics or very involved and intricate plots into dance form. He/she imagines these complex dances, and attempts to interpret them without any real knowledge or awareness of the technical problems which need to be addressed. A skilled dance composer has acquired this knowledge, and understands that it is an integral part of the craft. Through the experience of trial and error, a creative person endeavouring to compose dances gradually learns that knowledge of the limitations of the art form disciplines imagination to that which is possible.

– The Imagination and the Composer's Initial Reaction to the Stimulus –

MATERIAL CONTENT

On hearing a lively piece of music the composer, spontaneously or through meditation, consciously recalls movements which pertain to the quality of liveliness. This response may occur simultaneously with movement if the composer improvises immediately with the music, or it may occur solely within the thought of the composer while listening to the music.

The composer's initial reaction to the stimulus thus evokes certain conscious ideas or mental images but these do not come from 'out of the blue', for as Redfern (1973) states:

> To be imaginative in the aesthetic realm demands knowledge and understanding of the standards and techniques peculiar to the art form in question. (p. 20)

The conscious recall of suitable movements for communication of liveliness occurs within the imagination of the composer. He/she imagines a dancer or dancers performing movements which he/she *knows* (knowledge) and which are within the range of acceptable vocabulary to depict the mood (understanding of the standards).

THE DANCE FORM

During or after this initial response to the music, and as a result of it, the composer may imagine a dance outcome. The outcome, whether an entire framework or only a small part, continues to guide the composer's movement response to the stimulus. The outcome might, for example, be seen to grow to a height in the middle when the lively dance would contain extravagant jumps, turns, rolls and leaps. It might also be imagined to have a final leap which exits from the stage. The composer, with this in mind, then begins to manipulate material to fit these conscious images, and thus starts composing.

– *The Imagination During Composition* –

MATERIAL CONTENT

The composer continues to search for movements from his/her repertoire which are deemed suitable, and tries to make them as original (imaginative) as possible. Perhaps this is achieved by altering the more commonly employed movement characteristics, such as, size, level, direction, part of body utilised, qualitative content and gesture. It is understandable that the composer should want to aim for originality in the sense of doing something that has not been done before. It is also understandable that he/she should wish to move away from conventional movement towards a form which is unique and his/her own. But the movements:

> ... can hardly be counted as original or imaginative if they occur without reference to existing practices, and without the understanding and deliberate intent which make a 'differing form' possible.   Redfern (1973), p. 15

This reinforces the comment made previously, that, however original, the vocabulary must be recognisable to be successful.

It can be open to many interpretations but these should be within a certain realm of ideas. We all look for imaginative or original movement material and evaluate dances with this as a criterion. The composer should set out with this aim. It may be that the dance demands to be stated simply, but the simplest movement content can be presented imaginatively by means of sensitive juxtapositioning or original and inspired use of repetition.

THE DANCE FORM

As soon as the first motif is composed, the imagined dance outcome becomes clearer in form. The composer begins to think of possible directions that it may take. For example, he/she may imagine:

a) an immediate repetition of the motif developed and varied, followed by an introduction of a new and contrasting motif, or

b) an introduction of another motif, as contrast to the first, followed by an interplay of the two.

According to experience, the composer, consciously or intuitively, employs the elements of form – repetition, variation, contrast, climax, proportion, balance, transition, logical development and unity. He/she may imagine some of these elements within the dance form before actually manipulating the material. He/she may, for example, consciously imagine the climax movements and work up to these through logical sequencing of the material content and placing of the dancers within the stage space. This belies a mainstream approach, of course. Alternative approaches (see Section 2: *Methods of Construction 8*) require just as much imaginative thought in the choreographic process.

It would seem, therefore, that the images construed within the composer's thought pose compositional problems and that these require further imaginative thought in order to solve them. This latter imaginative or original thought might produce even richer form than that imagined in the initial stages. The saying goes, 'Let your imagination run away with you'. Often this occurs, and the composer may experience surprise with the results in composition. This element of surprise is as pertinent during the process of composition as it is in the viewing of it as a completed form:

A work of art always surprises us: *it has worked its effect before we have become conscious of its presence.*

Read (1931), p. 69

During composition, the composer's imagination is structured by the stimulus, by knowledge of movement material and, above all, by the 'technique peculiar to' dance construction. But within this framework there is freedom and the range and quality of the imagination used have a great deal to do with the ultimate success of the dance.

– *Intuition* –

In building up his composition, the artist may proceed intellectually or instinctively, or perhaps more often partly by one method and partly by the other. But most of the great artists of the Renaissance – Piero della Francesca, Leonardo, Raphael – had a definite bias towards an intellectual construction, often based, like Greek sculpture or architecture, on a definite mathematical ratio. But when we come to Baroque composition like El Greco's 'Conversion of St. Maurice' the scheme is so intricate, so amazing in its repeated relations, so masterly in the reinforcement which gives form to intention, that the form itself, as often the solution of some mathematical problem, must have been an intuition.   Read (1931), p. 62

Although Read suggests that some great artists proceed either intellectually or instinctively, it is accepted by many that, in dance, the composer *must* allow intuition to guide him/her. At the same time he/she always needs to intellectualise because, during the process of composition, it is important continually to evaluate, select and memorise the movement content. The question is whether intuition is the main method of procedure, and how it is supported by knowledge which, for the dance composer, includes knowledge of movement and material and methods of constructing dance form.

INTUITION WITHOUT KNOWLEDGE

The composer who relies mostly on intuition may produce something that is good and instinctively recognise it as such:

> It is recognised that the inspiration and conception of a work of art may often derive from the unconscious levels of the artist's personality and may not lie wholly open to deliberate, conscious apprehension. Hence the created work may embody fuller wealth of import than the artist himself is aware of. Indeed it is sometimes maintained that the artist himself is not the best interpreter or exponent of his work.   Osborne (1968), p. 188

If the art work derives from the unconscious, without the support of knowledge, the form that emerges through intuition may only be successful once or even twice. Here the artist has hit upon something accidentally but, without knowledge of form, cannot begin to estimate why it is good and so never progresses beyond trial and error methods. In this situation, the composer experiences great frustration if he/she cannot be successful again and does not know why.

KNOWLEDGE OVERRULING INTUITION

The composer who treats composition as an academic exercise often produces work which lacks feeling and warmth of human expression. The form may be sound theoretically but too predictable, and the content might lack the excitement that often derives from intuitive artistic flair.

INTUITION WITH KNOWLEDGE

The middle line, of course, is the best route. The composer's natural feeling or artistry needs to be disciplined by knowledge and 'techniques peculiar to the art form'. For example, knowledge of principles of form guides the composer's intuitive inspiration whilst he/she is shaping the dance:

> These structural motives are very important in the making of a picture or any other plastic work of art, though they are not necessarily a deliberate choice of the artist.
>   Read (1931), p. 69

The more one works with principles the more they become a part of one's technique. The dance composer who has consciously manipulated the principles of form for long enough, will find that they become part of his/her sub-conscious. To some extent, the methods of constructing a dance will instinctively incorporate consideration of the elements of form. This is what Read may be implying when he says 'they are not necessarily a deliberate choice of the artist'. The artist's intuition is disciplined by the sub-conscious knowledge of form. But the intuition should be 'let loose' because the unique personal qualities which each work of art must possess can only emerge through the personal contribution of the artist and his/her intuitive feeling for art.

INTUITION AND ACQUAINTANCE KNOWLEDGE
The composer who engages in use of resources as discussed in Section 3 will inevitably learn from them. If he/she has frequent opportunity to see dance in the theatre or study it as repertoire, he/she may gradually become perceptive of form, style and meaning and sub-consciously absorb a feeling for these elements which can be transposed into his/her own works. This learning can be acquired gradually through experience, but it is accelerated greatly if the composer has knowledge of form, style and meaning, per se. The student-composer who is in the process of learning about composition will be able to appraise critically what is seen within a clear frame of reference. The student without such knowledge appraises through feeling alone.

Experience of watching varied dance works and encountering works of other art forms, is perhaps a means of developing intuitive awareness and, even though it might not be a conscious awareness, the composer is bound to acquire an acquaintance knowledge of form which enhances his/her potential in dance composition.

Theoretical knowledge, supported by acquaintance knowledge of form, disciplines and guides the composer's intuition, but feeling must be allowed to penetrate and have an effect upon the work.

– *Knowing and Feeling* –

At best, the composer is knowledgeable in terms of material for dance and methods of constructing a dance. He/she is also an experienced viewer of dances and has what is deemed a good imagination and a feeling for dance as art.

Knowledge of principles of composition and acquaintance knowledge of form, style and meaning in dance may be kept at a voluntary conscious level, or it might be so ingrained that it functions at the involuntary sub-conscious level. Imagination and intuition, inextricably interwoven with, and guided by, knowledge provide the bounds of the composer's freedom.

The inspirational moments always require intellectual evaluation and analysis so that they may properly fit into the form of the dance, but the rarity of the moments themselves is inexplicable. The composer is constantly moving from feeling to knowing or the other way round. Somehow feeling and knowing merge on an indefinable plane. Discussion on this aspect of the compositional process can only go so far. However much is said, it remains but the 'tip of the iceberg'.

The important point here is that, whilst recognising the essential roles of imagination and intuition, it must also be clear that there exists a body of knowledge sufficient to guide and structure the movement outcomes of 'feeling and imagining' into order and form.

The chart on page 144 may be taken to represent a summary of the discussion presented so far.

There is no distinct order of events during the process of composition. The curved arrow indicates a general direction, though there is bound to be a return to a particular stage at any time. For example, up until the last movement is selected the composer constantly needs to improvise and explore a range of possibilities.

– *Evaluations* –

Response to a work of art is always based on prior experience which may grow to become discerning and mature. A dance can only be measured as successful in a relative sense. Relative to the onlooker's experience and background and the composer's stage of development in composing.

THE PROCESS OF COMPOSITION IN DANCE

COMPOSITION

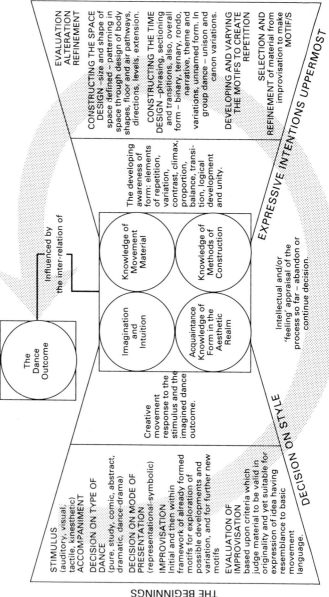

EXPRESSIVE INTENTIONS UPPERMOST

EVALUATION
ALTERATION
REFINEMENT

CONSTRUCTING THE SPACE
DESIGN –size and shape of
space defined – patterning in
space through design of body
shapes, floor and air pathways,
directions, levels, extension.

CONSTRUCTING THE TIME
DESIGN –phrasing, sectioning
and transitions; also, overall
form – binary, ternary, rondo,
narrative, theme and
variations; unnamed form. In
group dance – unison and
canon variations.

DEVELOPING AND VARYING
THE MOTIFS TO CREATE
REPETITION

SELECTION AND
REFINEMENT of material from
improvisation to make
MOTIF/S

The developing
awareness of
form: elements
of repetition,
variation,
contrast, climax,
balance, transi-
tion, logical
development
and unity.

Knowledge of
Movement
Material

Knowledge of
Methods of
Construction

Imagination
and
Intuition

Acquaintance
Knowledge of
Form in the
Aesthetic
Realm

Influenced by
the inter-relation of

The
Dance
Outcome

Intellectual and/or
'feeling' appraisal of the
process so far – abandon or
continue decision.

DECISION ON STYLE

Creative
movement
response to the
stimulus and the
imagined dance
outcome.

STIMULUS
(auditory, visual;
tactile, kinesthetic)
ACCOMPANIMENT

DECISION ON TYPE OF
DANCE
(pure, study, comic, abstract,
dramatic; dance-drama)

DECISION ON MODE OF
PRESENTATION
(representational-symbolic)

IMPROVISATION
Initial and then within
framework of already formed
motifs for exploration of
possible developments and
variation, and for further new
motifs

EVALUATION OF
IMPROVISATION
based upon criteria which
judge material to be valid in
originality and yet suitable for
expression of idea having
resemblance to basic
movement
language.

THE BEGINNINGS

There is no objective formula for evaluation of a dance. It cannot be entirely processed by factual analysis, yet it is not merely judged on inner feelings or personal taste. Inevitably the onlooker will reflect intellectually about what is seen and, in viewing art, this is always influenced by aesthetic judgments:

> The word aesthetic comes from the Greek word, 'aesthesis' which means 'to perceive or to look at objects of interest'.
> Curl (1973), p. 23

Looking at something to appreciate and describe it aesthetically implies that we use:

> ... concepts of shape, pattern, form, design; these then are the concepts appropriate to the aesthetic form of awareness, they connote perceptual characteristics.
> Curl (1973), p. 23

Most of us can appreciate an art work aesthetically but probably lack the ability to describe it. That which is aesthetically pleasing will *seem* right, significant, complete, balanced and unified, and we may *feel* these qualities rather than *know* them. Of course, each onlooker will perceive something different, but aesthetic evaluation will have much to do with the form of the dance. Some viewers might see the intricate shaping and changes of the designs of the dancers in relation to each other as being the most aesthetically pleasing aspect of the dance. Others might appreciate the quality of the dancers' movements, and the patterns into which these have been designed. A few may be pleased by the overall shape of the dance, and see the beginning, middle and end in proportionate relationship, and each section as a well balanced entity yet carefully blended into a unified whole. Others may feel a sense of pleasure on recognition of the repetitions and contrasts and follow the design of the dance within these frames of reference.

It could be that the emotional intensity of the dance completely immersed the viewer so that, after the experience, he/she remembered little of its form, only that it felt right at the time. Here, the viewer has been less aesthetically and more dramatically moved with the dance. But one could say that the drama does not come across as significant unless embodied into a suitable shape, design or form.

It would appear, therefore, that aesthetic evaluation is to do with the onlooker's perception of the dance as a work of art having form, beauty and meaning. This is always accompanied by an inner and immeasurable appreciation of form in art which has grown for the viewer by virtue of experience in the total world of art, through pictures, poems, plays, films, sculptures, music as well as dance.

Intellectual reflection requires factual analysis which can occur only if there is knowledge. The critic might judge more objectively from this standpoint though there are no set criteria by which one dance can be judged against another. Each dance uses material and is constructed in a different way from every other dance, and this makes comparison in judgment a very difficult task. Nevertheless, intellectual reflection upon the following lines might be possible.

CONSIDER THE WHOLE DANCE AS A WORK OF ART

1. Has the composer reached the objective? Did the dance seem significant and worth watching, or was it obscure and meaningless?
2. Did the dance have continuity? Did it sustain interest throughout or were there some weak parts?
3. Was every part of the dance essential to the whole?
4. Was the style of the dance clearly established and then maintained throughout?
5. Was there enough depth and variety in the material content or was it too simple, naive and predictable?
6. Was the construction of the dance seen to have unity through its rhythmic structure?
7. Was there an element of surprise or was it all too easy to follow?
8. Was the choice of music – or other stimulus for accompaniment – suitable for the theme of the dance?
9. Was the dance constructed with an understanding of the stimulus?

After consideration of the dance as a whole art work, the student of dance composition might persist further in intellectual reflection. There is more to a dance than its 'pieces' but these can be extracted and assessed. The following questions may help in this process.

1. Consider the dance idea

a) Was the basic idea behind the dance conveyed, only partly conveyed, or not conveyed at all?

b) Were the movement images translatable?

c) Did the form aid understanding of the underlying theme?

d) Was the idea easily perceived or did the onlooker have to search intently to find meaning, and indeed, perhaps read into it that which was not meant to be?

e) Was the topic too deep and involved for translation into dance movement?

f) Simple ideas conveyed with artistry and originality often make the most successful dances. In pursuit of originality, however, has the composer chosen material which is too obscure in relation to the idea and, therefore, lost the simplicity by over-elaboration?

g) Is it worth dancing about? Does it merit artistic expression? Does it have significance in the modern world?

h) Does it cause emotional response and arouse the senses?

i) Is the communication based on an individual distillation of expression or a hackneyed set of clichés?

2. Consider the movement content

a) Did the composer choose 'right' movements in relation to the idea?

b) Was there a width of movement content which created variety and interest?

c) Was there balance of action, qualitative, space and relationship emphasis or too much concentration on any one?

d) Were the movements easily discernable as symbolic or representative of meaningful communication?

ACTION

e) Were the actions made interesting by varied co-ordinations and juxtapositioning?

f) Was the range of actions enough for the dance? (A range limited to nearly all gesture and positioning into body shape is a common fault.)

QUALITIES

g) Was there enough qualitative or dynamic variation in the dance?

h) Did the qualities colour the actions with appropriate light and shade enhancing the meaning?

SPACE

i) Was the spatial aspect of the movement relevant to the idea?

j) Did the composer utilise the stage space to best advantage and with consideration of locality and its expressive connotations?

k) Was the dance an interesting visual experience creating lines and shapes in space in harmony with the idea?

l) Was the use of focus a noticeable feature and did it communicate the intention?

m) Were the movements extended in space enough for the audience to appreciate them?

RELATIONSHIP

n) Were there enough dancers or too many for the idea?

o) Did the group relationship come over successfully?

p) Was the unison achieved?

q) Were the individuals placed advantageously in the group for the visual effect, or were some members masked by other dancers at any time?

r) Did the design of the group in terms of complementing body shapes, levels, and complementing movement patterns, emerge as successful and meaningful in the dance?

s) Did the solo stand out as important in the presence of the ground bass, or did it diminish by virtue of sheer strength of numbers in the preceding and following sections?

t) Was the number of dancers absolutely necessary at all times, or were there moments when the duos could have been solos and the trios could have been duos, etc?

3. Consider the construction elements of form

a) Motif: Were the motifs apparent and foundational to the rest of the content of the dance?

b) Repetition: Was there enough repetition to establish the meanings in the chosen movements or was repetition over-stressed?

c) Variety and Contrast: Did the dance utilise variety and contrast in the best and most appropriate ways, or was contrast just put in for its own sake without due reference to the total meaning?

d) Climax or Highlights: How did the climaxes or highlights emerge? Were they apparent or forceful enough?

e) Transition: Did the transitions merge into and become part of the whole and were they effectively employed as links between parts?

f) Proportion and Balance: Was the dance balanced in terms of content or did one section appear irrelevant? Was one section too long and the other too short? Were they too much of the same length? Did the sections have interesting differences?

g) Logical Development: Was the whole dance easy to follow? Did the idea emerge in a logical way, or were there many sudden changes in content confusing the issue? Did the end really emerge as important with a clear enough build-up, or was it left suspended?

h) Unity: Did the whole become formed and a unified manifestation of the idea? Did the dance appear well constructed, each part having its role to play in forming a relevant, meaningful and artistic whole shape (which may be categorised as binary, or ternary or rondo, etc.)?

4. Consider the style
a) Was the style selected suitable in expressing the theme?
b) Was the dance coherent in style?
c) Is the style relevant in today's dance context?
d) In the event of the task requiring specific replication of a style, e.g. composed in Graham style or in Rock 'n' Roll style, is there sufficient understanding of and adherence to the details of the specified style.
e) If the task did not require specific replication of a known style, was there sufficient originality in use of the style or was it a direct copy of a known style without the composer's own 'signature'?
f) Were the performers able to present the style with sufficient clarity?

5. Consider the performance
a) Did the dancer's performance enrich or negate the dance composition?
b) Was the performer sincere and involved in the rendering?
c) Were the required technical skills mastered to the enhancement of the dance or did technical deficiency ruin the composition?
d) Did the performer make real the images and movement content according to the composer's wishes or did personal interpretation alter the intention to some degree?

e) Did the performers dance with a view to a communicative presentation to an audience or were they too involved within themselves, or the group, to make this positive?

f) Was the style of the dance adhered to throughout its performance?

6. Consider the stimulus as initiation of the dance

a) Was the stimulus suitable for a dance to emerge from it?

b) Was it apparent as an origin of the dance or did its relevance become lost?

c) Was it viewed in a rich artistically imaginative way to stimulate an interesting dance or was it translated too literally or too slightly?

7. Consider the stimulus as accompaniment for dance

a) If it (e.g. pole, cloak, material) was manipulated by the dancer/s was this done with ease and clarity or did it seem too difficult to manage?

b) Did the accompanying object cause a lack of movement from the dancer/s?

c) Was the accompanying stimulus too large or too much in itself rendering the dancer as minute and insignificant ? (A film moving on the wall behind the dancers, for instance.)

d) If music was used as accompaniment:

   i) Did it fit with the dance idea?

   ii) Was it cut and abused for the purpose of the dance and therefore not valid or appropriate?

   iii) Did the composer use the phrasing in the music or ignore it?

   iv) Was the music too powerful or too slight for the dance? (A solo danced to an orchestral symphony, or a large dramatic group dance danced to a piano solo piece, for instance.)

   v) Was the structure of the music in time suitably employed by the composer? (If a beat or 'pop' piece was used for instance, it would be unwise to move to every beat, on the other hand, if a piece is in strict $\left[{}^4_4\right]$ time it would be inadvisable to swoop, swirl and move continuously through the beat.)

   vi) Was the music really necessary and an inseparable part of the dance?

8. Consider the other staging facets

a) Was the decor/lighting relevant to the idea?
b) Did the decor/lighting enhance the dance or overpower it?
c) Were the props placed correctly and did they have enough use to merit their presence?
d) Were the costumes relevant to the idea and the style of the dance?
e) Could the performers move easily without limitation in the costumes?
f) Was the make-up an enhancing feature?
g) Did any of the staging facets detract from the dance itself?

This list of questions, although extensive, is by no means exhaustive. Furthermore, it would be a cold and almost tortuous process to analyse and evaluate a dance by asking *all* these questions.

Inextricably bound with intellectual reflection on any level are the feelings of pleasure that an aesthetic work of art evokes in an onlooker. Each person experiences this pleasure in varying ways and in different degrees, but – in judging art – it is the fundamental criterion. Above all, therefore, the most important question to ask the viewer and the composer in relation to his/her own work, is whether or not the work was pleasing. *Did you like it?* If the answer is yes, there is, perhaps, no need for further evaluation, except that it can become a useful learning process to understand why it was appreciated. If the answer is no, then probably, reasons for its 'failure' can be found by asking *some* of the questions.

The teacher of dance composition would perhaps find the questions a useful frame of reference for constructively criticising a student's attempt in composition, but mentioning only the most salient points. Also, students of composition could, perhaps, criticise their own and other students' work by such questioning.

For the composer, such evaluations can only be made in retrospect and, probably, only after a period of time has elapsed since the completion of the dance. Personal satisfaction or dissatisfaction is the initial feeling of a composer, who may find that it is necessary to stand back from the actual experience in order to become more objective.

A last evaluation

In the final analysis, a dance performance succeeds in generating enthusiasm when the audience is aesthetically stirred. It fails if an audience remains unmoved and unresponsive because feelings are left dormant.

An understanding of the 'rules' discovered through analytical essay and mastery of the craft of composition, helps towards the production of successful dances. When this understanding is combined with the composer's creative inspiration, born of imagination, intuition, artistry and vision, the dance will probably possess the elusive 'something' which assures successful impact.

– Conclusion –

This book has taken a close look at objectives, content, methods and evaluation in dance composition, and strongly suggests that theories, though necessary, are meant to be working statements. As Dewey (1946) expressed it:

> They are not meant to be ideas frozen into absolute standards masquerading as eternal truth or programs rigidly adhered to; rather, theory is to serve as a guide in systematising knowledge . . .

Theory is practical in that it provides a guide for action. It clarifies and structures the processes of thought. Practice in adherence to a set of guidelines or principles will structure the process of thought that goes with the practical action of making a dance, but it is important to acknowledge that, in art, the guidelines are never fixed. There is no particular set which will predetermine a specific dance, or guarantee a successful outcome. It is certain, however, that the gifted composer, who may claim to work through insight only, has already assimilated the theory behind the practice.

The acquisition of concepts and their application in a discipline such as the art of making dances demand much time and diligent study. Learning is aided if the subject matter is structured from the simple to the complex. Experience of this kind can lead to the development of an ability to compose, but this demands a grasp of the interwoven nature of theory and practice. It is impossible to learn to compose dances by reading alone. In today's technology environment, much can be added to the written word. Section 3 of this book attempts to illustrate how teaching and learning in dance will become revolutionised through an integration of visual moving dance resources combined with text – on paper, on screen, or accessed via the Internet. In this way, knowledge gained from study of professionally choreographed dance works will 'put flesh on the bones' of theory learned from textbooks such as this and from the students' own practical composition classes.

This relationship between theory and practice can work in both directions, of course. The dance composer, constantly trying to relate theory and practice, faces a maze-like problem. Theory, in a book such as this, can provide clear signposts in a journey of discovery towards making dances that have form and clarity of expression. A consideration of the nature of these signposts and their regulating effect upon the work of the developing composer has been made in this book.

SECTION 5

Practical Assignments for Students

The following examples offer ideas for exploration in relation
to the text in Sections 1, 2 and 3.

Instructions are progressively staged. After each assignment,
suggestions which may be helpful will be found.

Reference to a particular part of the text is given with each
assignment but this only indicates an emphasis. The student-
composer should constantly strive to integrate all aspects of the
process of composition as far as he/she is able but, for study
purposes, he/she may choose to make a dance stressing one
facet. Indeed it is important that he/she attempts to solve
different compositional problems each time a composition is
made. In this way, the composer may gradually grow to understand the many contributory factors of expression and form
which make dances works of art.

Many of these example assignments could be linked with a
choice of stimulus. Some of the frameworks for composition
might therefore be used several times with different stimuli. The
student-composer should also endeavour to make dances of
various styles – styles indigenous to countries, personal styles
of choreographers, styles of different periods in history, and, of
course, styles of different dance forms (e.g. contemporary,
classical ballet, jazz, social).

– *Improvisation* –

ACTION PHRASE: **travel, turn, open, close, stretch**

Keep the sequence order but explore different ways of performing the actions. The exploration should stay within *action.*

Reference: Section 1, Movement and Meaning

1) Different ways to *travel:*
   a) using a variety of parts of the feet to take weight,
   b) leading with a variety of body parts into steps,
   c) step patterns (skips, hops, runs, gallops, slides, formed into repetitive sequences),
   d) on other body parts,
   e) on different body parts successively,
   f) emphasising bend, stretch or twist,
   g) adding jump and/or gestures and/or turns.

2) Different ways of *turning:*
   a) on both feet,
   b) from one foot to the other,
   c) on one foot,
   d) pivoting or spinning,
   e) jumping, hopping,
   f) inwards or outwards accompanied by arm and/or leg gestures,
   g) led by different parts of the body,
   h) on different parts of the body,
   i) transferring weight during the turn onto different body parts.

3) Different ways of *opening, closing and stretching:*
   a) symmetrically or asymmetrically,
   b) with simultaneous or successive flow,
   c) with parts of body isolated or with the whole body,
   d) led by different body parts,
   e) near or far and various degrees within the range,
   f) with transference of weight or jumping.

– *Improvisation* –

ACTION PHRASE: *travel, turn, open, close, stretch*

Keep the sequence order but explore different ways of performing it emphasising *quality* variations.

Reference: Section 1. Movement and Meaning

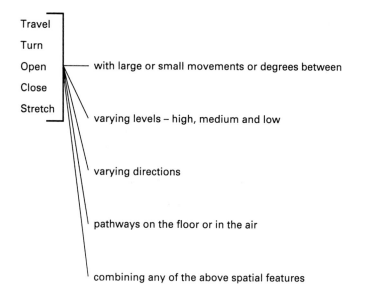

Travel
Turn
Open
Close
Stretch

with large or small movements or degrees between

varying levels – high, medium and low

varying directions

pathways on the floor or in the air

combining any of the above spatial features

– *Improvisation* –

ACTION PHRASE: **travel, turn, open, close, stretch**

Keep the sequence order but explore different ways of performing it emphasising *quality* variations.

Reference: Section 1. Movement and Meaning

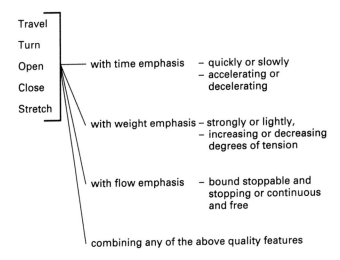

Travel
Turn
Open
Close
Stretch

— with time emphasis — – quickly or slowly
     – accelerating or
      decelerating

with weight emphasis – strongly or lightly,
     – increasing or decreasing
      degrees of tension

with flow emphasis — – bound stoppable and
     stopping or continuous
     and free

combining any of the above quality features

– *Explorations in Movement and Meaning* –

Use each of the following phrases to express a different idea. Try to find more than one idea for each phrase.

Reference: Section 1. Movement and Meaning

ACTION PHRASES

PHRASE 1
Rise . . .
Travel . . .
Close . . .
Fall . . .
Open . . .

PHRASE 2
Gesture leading into turn . . .
Travel into balance . . .
Tip into transference of weight . . .
Stretch and rise . . .
Travel and leap . . .

PHRASE 3
Leg gesture into stepping . . .
Open and turn . . .
Stand still . . .
Isolate and move three body parts in succession . . .
Curl . . .
Arm gesture into twist . . .

1) The student should attempt to define each idea by differentiation of the action content.

2) The accompanying qualitative content should alter within the phrase and be selected with a different emphasis for each of the ideas.

3) Each idea will also influence the way the space is used.

– *Explorations in Movement and Meaning* –

Use each of the following phrases to express a different idea. Try to find more than one idea for each phrase.

Reference: Section 1. Movement and Meaning

QUALITY PHRASES

PHRASE 1
From firm tension gradually lose tension to become light . . .
Move quickly and lightly . . .
Relax three parts of the body successively . . .
Become firm . . .
Release all tension and collapse . . .

PHRASE 2
Move freely and continuously . . .
Move with hesitation – holding back . . .
Make a series of sudden movements . . .
Travel quickly, and freely to end in sudden and strong stillness . . .

PHRASE 3
Move lightly and slowly . . .
Move slowly with changing tensions . . .
Move quickly alternating between firm tension and light qualities . . .
Spin accelerating and decelerating to end in a strong held position . . .

The context of the expression must be adhered to throughout the phrase. The quality changes should seem logical within the chosen contexts. The mover's use of space and action should enhance the expression and add interest to each phrase.

– *Explorations in Movement and Meaning* –

Use each of the following phrases to express a different idea.
Try to find more than one idea for each phrase.

Reference: Section 1. Movement and Meaning

SPATIAL PHRASES

PHRASE 1
Move with a constantly changing focus . . .
Move with a fixed focus . . .
Change focus and then move . . . repeat this three times . . .
Focus on one body part and move into different directions . . .
Focus high and then low . . .

PHRASE 2
Start with very small movements and increase in size to very
large . . .
Move with very large movements . . .
Alternately move one side of the body with small gestures and
the other side with large gestures . . .
Intersperse large and small movements . . .
Finish with one movement which gradually expands from a
small shape to a large shape, or, the reverse . . .

PHRASE 3
Start in the centre of the dance area, move backwards to centre
back . . .
Move in a series of curves to end centre front . . .
Move slightly right and then left . . .
Move on a wide circular pathway to the right and end in the
left back corner . . .
Move diagonally across the space from the left back corner to
the right front corner . . .
Move backwards towards the centre and then exit from one of
the four corners to the expression . . .

The context of the expression must be adhered to throughout
the phrase. The spatial changes should seem relevant within the
chosen contexts. The mover's use of action and quality should
enhance the expression and add interest to the phrases.

– *Explorations in Movement and Meaning* –

Relationship through group shapes and numerical variations.

Reference: Section 2. *Methods of Construction 3*

1) FOR A GROUP OF THREE
Start in a closed circle . . .
Become scattered and unrelated . . .
Dancer 1 move to dancer 2 . . .
Dancers 1 and 2 move to dancer 3 . . .
Move in a closed line . . .
Move to spread the line . . .
Make the line into a file and move . . .
Dancers 1 and 2 surround dancer 3 . . .
Make a circle . . .
Become very close and in contact with each other . . .
Select an appropriate ending . . .

Decide on a dance idea suitable for this framework and select movement content for composition.

2) FOR A GROUP OF FOUR:
Create a framework as above stressing symmetry in group shape and numerical arrangement.
Decide on a dance idea suitable for this framework and select movement content for composition.

3) FOR A GROUP OF SEVEN:
Create a framework stressing asymmetry in group shape and numerical arrangement.
Decide on a dance idea suitable for this framework and select movement content for composition.

1) The dance idea will define the action, and spatial content which should be compatible with the set group shapes and numerical relationships.

2) The created frameworks should contain a variety of group shapes and numerical arrangements. Too much variety, however, would lead to confused and unconnected happenings.

3) Each group shape and numerical arrangement can be retained for varying lengths of time in the dance. (One may be kept for several phrases of movement and another could be used only transitorily.)

4) As additional challenge for advanced students, consideration of the use of the stage space in relation to a specified 'front' might be included.

– Explorations in Movement and Meaning –

RELATIONSHIP THROUGH GROUND PATTERN AND NUMERICAL ARRANGEMENTS FOR SIX OR MORE DANCERS:

1) On paper, make a series of diagrams which show ground patterns and numerical arrangements inviting a variety of relationships.

2) Select a dance idea which suits the use of the spatial and relationship framework.

3) Compose a dance selecting appropriate movement content and using the set ground patterns and numerical arrangements.

Reference: Section 2. *Methods of Construction 3*

1) The ground pattern should use all the space available and consist of a mixture of design, such as curves, straight lines and angles. The dancers should be numerically divided in many ways and the spatial positioning of each dancer should be clearly shown on the ground pattern diagrams.

2) The dance idea will define the action and quality content. While the floor patterning and numerical relationship is set, the other aspects of spatial design (group shape, levels, directions, focus) and relationships (face to face, back to back, in contact, surrounding) can be selected to fit the idea.

3) The idea and the set framework should be compatible and merge into a meaningful dance form.

– *Improvisation* –

Hover
Twist
Swirl
Skim
Lift
Dip
Fall   Explore some of these words as stimuli.
Circle   Improvise and then compose motifs to depict
Sway   one of the following ideas:

Movement of the Wind   A Fairground
Movement of the Sea   Lost
Movement of Birds   Insanity

Reference: Section 1. Material Content

The action words have rhythmic characteristics and, therefore, have an implied quality content.

Linking them in different orders will vary phrase rhythms and each idea will suggest certain patterns of juxtapositioning.

Further differentiation can be achieved through the spatial patterning (placing, direction, level, size, pathways) of the movements.

Before selecting material for the motifs, the solo dancer might improvise for some time changing the order of the word stimuli.

Further exploration in twos or groups might extend the range of interpretation implicit in the words.

– *Composition* –

MOTIF AND DEVELOPMENT

1) Use a simple action motif such as:
   a) side and close,
or b) sway right and left,
or c) four walks,
or d) a waltz step,
and develop it in *action* increasing the complexity until it is as full as possible involving a multiplicity of body parts.

2) Make a study showing the simple beginning, an increase in complexity, a decrease in complexity and a return to the beginning motif.

Reference: Section 2. *Methods of Construction 2*

1) The following developments might be incorporated:
   a) taking weight on various parts of the feet,
   b) leading with various parts of the feet or other body parts,
   c) emphasising bend, stretch and/or twist,
   d) adding arm and/or leg gestures, also gestures of other body parts,
   e) transferring weight on to other body parts,
   f) adding jumps,
   g) adding turns,
   h) emphasising travel,
   i) changing body shapes.

2) The progression towards the climax might well retain parts of the original motif. The climax reached through a steady build-up in complexity should show a richness of action derived from the original motif but at this point the original motif will not be visible.

– *Composition* –

MOTIF AND DEVELOPMENT

1) Use a simple action motif such as:
   a) side and close step,
or b) gesture, step, waltz step,
or c) gesture, turn, sway right and left,
or d) two steps into leg and arm gesture,
and develop it *qualitatively* increasing the complexity until it is as full as possible.

2) Make a study showing a simple beginning, an increase in complexity, a decrease in complexity and a return to the beginning motif.

Reference: Section 2. *Methods of Construction 2*

1) The following developments might be incorporated:
   a) emphasis on one quality, e.g. speed, changing with each repetition of the whole motif, or changing during the motif,
   b) emphasis on two qualities, e.g. speed and force, changing with each repetition of the whole motif or changing during the motif,
   c) emphasis on three qualities, e.g. speed, force and continuity, changing with each repetition of the whole motif, or changing during the motif.

2) The motif should be given qualitative identity to start with and then developments can be seen as changes while the action remains the same.

– *Composition* –

MOTIF AND DEVELOPMENT

1) Use a simple action motif such as:
   a) side and close step with arm gesture
then b) sway right and left   ″   ″   ″
then c) four walks   ″   ″   ″
then d) waltz steps   ″   ″   ″
and develop it *spatially* increasing the complexity until it is full in spatial terms.

2) Make a short solo study showing the simple beginning, an increase in complexity, a decrease in complexity and a return to the beginning motif.

Reference: Section 2. *Methods of Construction 2*

1) The following developments might be incorporated:
   a) varying the size and/or level of actions,
   b) varying the directions of the steps of the whole motif or parts of the motif – also stressing different directions in other body parts,
   c) taking the action on different pathways – curves or straight lines – to make a variety of floor patterns.

2) The motif should have a spatial identity to start with, for instance, side and close and sway right and left stresses the side direction; although the arm gesture may take a different direction, the walks naturally take a forward direction and the waltz step contains rise and fall or up and down movement. These spatial aspects can be changed while the action remains identifiable throughout.

– *Composition* –

1) Go through the possible developments and variations of the action of a side and close step as detailed in *Methods of Construction 2*

2) In twos: structure a short dance based upon this motif with
either   a court-like style
or   a comic flavour

Reference: Section 2. *Methods of Construction 2*

The characteristics given to the starting side and close must be retained for long enough and then followed logically by another way of performing side and close. Use about four or five ways only with developments on these.

The duo relationship should be varied and interesting.

– *Composition* –

MOTIF, DEVELOPMENT AND VARIATION FOR A SOLO

1) a) Compose a phrase motif to approximately 16 bars of music.
   b) Repeat it exactly but emphasising the other side of the body.
   c) Develop and vary it spatially.
   d) Develop and vary its quality content.
   e) Develop and vary its action content by simultaneously combining more actions with the original actions.
   f) Develop and vary the phrase so that the space, quality and action content are slightly altered throughout.
   g) Extract a small part of the motif and repeat it in four different ways.
   h) Repeat the original phrase in a different order.

2) Select 4 or 5 of the above phrases and link them to compose a study form.

Reference: Section 2. *Methods of Construction 2*

The phrases could be linked so that the developments occur end on or simultaneously. The study should be a whole shape, each part leading naturally to the next.

– *Composition* –

1) Improvise with literal movement to show one of the following moods:
   a) boredom,
   b) carefree and frivolous,
   c) frustrated anger.

2) Select several movements and transform them into symbolic movements.

3) Make a phrase motif linking the movements into a logical order.

4) Repeat the motif with developments.

Reference: Section 2. *Methods of Construction 1 and 2*

1) The improvisation should be within a range of movement normally associated with the 'everyday' expression of the moods.

2) The actions might then be transformed by enlargement, (increase in size – the movement involving more of the body – extending further in space) performing it with a different body part/s, emphasising or altering its rhythmic structure, adding more action (e.g. jumps added to the shaking fist action for anger). All this results in development and variation of the original representative movement. The degree of development or variation will determine the movement as 'mostly representative' or 'most symbolic'.

3) The repetition should extend even further towards symbolic presentation.'

– *Composition* –

1) a) Start with four walks forward.
   b) Change the rhythm.
   c) Retain b) and add a leg gesture to one of the walks.
   d) Retain b) & c) and add an arm gesture to one of the walks.
   e) Retain b) c) & d) and add a turn to one of the walks.
   f) Retain b) c) d) & e) and add a jump to one of the walks.
   g) Retain b) c) d) e) & f) and add low level to one of the walks.
   h) Retain b) c) d) e) f) & g) and add weight on different parts of the feet where appropriate.

2) Take the final outcome (a rich four walk action motif) and use it as a basis for a dance – disintegrating it, extracting from it, altering its order, developing and varying its content.

Reference: Section 2. *Methods of Construction 2*

Once the motif has been made it should be put to one side.

The composer is advised to select a small part as a starting point and then allow the dance to grow logically.

The overall original motif may never be used in the completed dance but its pieces will provide a relationship of content throughout.

The dance could be further stimulated by an idea which might have occurred to the composer during the exploration of the four walks.

– *Composition* –

1) Make a floor pattern motif using straight lines.

2) Make a floor pattern motif using curved pathways.

3) Create step patterns which are suitable for the floor patterns and employ legato or sustained and staccato or sudden qualities to emphasise the angularity or curvature.

4) Compose a short solo study establishing the material as follows:
  a) floor pattern using straight lines,
  b) floor pattern using curved lines,
  c) floor patterns with step patterns including defined qualities,
  d) developments and variations of c) amalgamating parts of the two patterns

Reference: Section 2. *Methods of Construction 2*

The study will become more complex in action and quality terms but the floor patterns should emerge as a constant and most important feature. They will appear more complex when parts of each are amalgamated.

– *Composition* –

MOTIF, DEVELOPMENT AND VARIATION FOR A DUO

1) Compose a *solo* phrase motif.

2) Use the phrase motif for two dancers – in unison using the same or complementary movements.

3) Repeat the phrase developing and varying the content and at some time employ canon using the same and complementary movements.

Reference: Section 2. *Methods of Construction 3*

1) If this assignment is given to two student-composers, both should learn and be able to dance the solo motif. This is then

adapted for composition of a duo, and the first phrase introduces the motif as material for two dancers.

2) The original motif should be performed by one or other of the dancers throughout this first phrase. In complementing, the student will naturally develop the original content. The development will be seen *at the same time* as the original.

3) The developments or variations of the original can be performed by both dancers in unison or canon.

– *Composition* –

MOTIF AND DEVELOPMENT FOR A GROUP (4–7)

1) Compose a solo motif lasting about 16 bars of music. Establish the motif for the group in unison.

2) Compose several repetitions of part or the whole of the motif emphasising variation within time (as illustrated on page 58) and include as many numerical divisions and spatial differentiations as possible.

Reference: Section 2. *Methods of Construction 2 and 3*

1) The motif can be split into parts, changed in order of its parts developed and varied by any means (action, quality, space or only by relationship).

2) The spatial and relationship design should enhance the presentation.

3) The orchestration in time should emerge as the prominent feature.

4) It will probably be found that the process requires a director 'out in front'.

5) There should not be too much going on at one time.

– *Composition* –

FOR THREE DANCERS

1) Work individually and make a phrase motif for one of the following characters:

> slow, gentle day-dreamer
> quick, lively, exuberant
> strong, forceful, dominating

2) Make a dance which successively brings each character to the foreground. Each character should perform his/her own phrase motif while the other two, through unison or canon background, copy, complement or contrast the motif but retain their individual characteristics.

Reference: Section 2. *Methods of Construction 3*

1) The three motifs should be contrasting in use of action, qualities and space.

2) The relationship of the three in terms of placing, focus and level should be interesting (the use of rostra could enhance the presentation).

3) While one character is performing the motif, the other two could complement, copy or contrast it, by doing the same movement but with different qualitative emphasis or, by developing and varying the movement (e.g. a slow gentle turn at medium level taken by the dreamy character could be accompanied by a fast double turn at high level performed by the quick, lively character and a firm travelling action on a circular pathway performed by the dominator) or, contrasting the movement with one from their own motifs. (This contrast should not occur too often since it is difficult to view, though intermittent previews or reviews of parts of motifs might be interesting.)

– *Composition* –

SOLO OR GROUP

1) Find a song or poem with a chorus and verse arrangement.

2) Make a motif for the chorus interpreting the mood and/or meaning of the words.

3) Make motifs for the verses trying to keep a sense of the changing meaning and yet retaining a movement relationship from verse to verse.

4) Make a dance in rondo form developing and varying the chorus' movement content each time in slightly different ways, taking care that they can follow and lead into each new verse.

Reference: Section 2. *Methods of Construction 2, 3 and 4*

1) The song or poem should be suitable for interpretation into dance.

2) The essence of meaning should emerge through the movement – some of the words might be clearly interpreted and others not at all. The accompaniment and dance should merge successfully – neither of them dominating the other.

3) The style or manner in which the movements in each chorus are performed should be adhered to throughout. The composer has the task of identifying the aspects of movement he/she wishes to retain in the verses to relate each one to the others. For instance, he/she may keep a 'swing' quality and use different actions and spatial patterns to keep to the context of the words.

4) The choruses should retain enough of the original to be clearly identified.

– *Composition* –

SOLO STUDY

1) Make two contrasting motifs.

2) Present the whole as A, B, then an amalgamation of A and B retaining the original content exactly, as far as possible.

3) Repeat an amalgam of A and B but with development and variation.

Reference: Section 2. *Methods of Construction 4* – binary form

1) The A and B motifs should be distinctive from each other.

2) In the first amalgamation it will be difficult to achieve logical development. The movements within each motif can be taken out of order. Some may not fit at all and, therefore, are best left out.

3) The second amalgamation could follow the order of the first but contain development and variation of the content.

– *Composition* –

TRANSITION
Given two short sequences of movement which are contrasted – make two different transitions to link them.

Reference: Section 2. *Methods of Construction 5*

Each transition should contain a flavour of both sequences.
One of them may be mostly repetitive of the first, intermittently introducing the second sequence. The other may retain only one aspect of the first, for instance, the quality content, while introducing the action and spatial content of the second.

– *Resource Based Learning into Composition* –

STYLE

Using video, study a section of choreography which you would call 'mainstream' contemporary dance and note which of the following stylistic features are evident:

- feet in parallel and all parts of the feet used sensitively
- trunk/centre of body important in all movements
- weight shifts into and out of balances
- contractions and release with upward focus
- tipping into and out of movements to achieve an ongoing feel
- hips initiating moves or extending beyond the centre line
- floorwork – moves into, across, on and out of floor
- natural opposition of arms and legs as in walking
- emphasis on qualities of swing, impulse and impact
- variety in length of phrases and rhythmic patterning

Select at least four of the above stylistic features and create a short solo study (2 minutes in duration) to perform to a colleague having given him/her the list first. Your colleague should then determine which four factors you emphasised and how you might improve your performance of them.

Reference: Section 2. *Methods of Construction 6*

The section of choreography on video should be short and permit the student to use slow motion, freeze frame and repetition of phrases.

The style in the student's own composition should be clearly defined and coherent.

– Resource Based Learning into Composition –

STYLE

Using video, select a section of choreography that you would label 'jazz' in style, e.g. Robert North's *Lonely Town, Lonely Street* (1984). Study it and note which of the following stylistic features are present:

- movements initiated and isolated to specific body parts e.g. hips, shoulders
- accented beats and syncopated rhythms
- downward stressed grounded movements
- sharp changes of direction and focus
- quick, short steps interspersed with long, smooth steps
- strong, sharp (percussive) contractions of centre of body and other body parts, e.g. elbows
- use of still held positions
- emphasis on use of knees to give different qualities
- emphasis of medium level in space

1) Copy the first phrase of the section and then add another phrase of your own to it retaining the stylistic features you noted from above.

2) Contrast these phrases with another phrase emphasising stylistic features which were not evident in the video section.

3) Link the two pieces of composition into A and B motifs and create a group dance for five based on them.

Reference: Section 2. *Methods of Construction 6*

1) The section of choreography on video should be a short solo and facilities for slow motion, freeze frame and repetition of it should be available to the students. They will probably need help in 'turning it around', i.e. copying the movements of a front facing dancer on the screen.

2) To fulfil this task students should have a suitable vocabulary of jazz movements. (A book such as *Modern Jazz Dance* by Dolores Kirton Cayou could be a helpful additional source here.)

3) The group dance should employ time and space design features (Section 2. *Methods of Construction 3*) and retain a coherence of jazz style.

– *Resource Based Learning into Composition* –

STYLE

Find a theme for a dance which requires you to distil the essence of an ethnic dance style and combine it with a Western contemporary or classical ballet style.

1) Research the ethnic dance style noting its distinctive characteristics, i.e. kinds of actions, qualities, spatial and relationship features.

2) View and study dance works of professional choreographers who have used an ethnic dance style in this way – e.g. Christopher Bruce's *Sergeant Early's Dream* (1986), *Ghost Dances* (1981) and *Cruel Garden* (1977), and Jiri Kylian's *Stamping Ground* (1982).

3) Work out ways in which you can combine the two dance styles to make an original combination of them and at the same time convey your idea.

Reference: Section 2. *Methods of Construction 6*

1) The research should, as far as it is possible, involve the student in studying the ethnic dance style at source, e.g. a particular form of African dance, South Asian (e.g. Bharatha Natyam), Aboriginal, Chinese. Study should include consideration of cultural influences on the dance style.

2) The viewing of dance works should be guided so that students can determine which characteristics derive from the ethnic form and which are Western in origin.

3) The student's work should show evidence of three styles merging – the ethnic, the Western and his or her own style.

– *Appreciation into Composition and Performance* –

RESOURCE-BASED TEACHING/LEARNING

Resource: *Intimate Pages* (1984) Choreographed by Christopher Bruce

Activity A: small group discussion – no more than five.

Video snippet – the beginning phrases up until the woman has stroked the man's head with her right hand. This should be available in isolation from the rest of the dance work and as an easily repeatable video resource.

1) Can you find two phrases and the beginning of a third phrase? What starts and ends each phrase?
2) What sort of feelings are the man and woman expressing?

Write down your answers to present to others.

═══════════

Activity B: study of choreography and practical composition task in twos.

Video snippet – same as above viewed several times as required.

1) Describe and list the spatial relationships between the dancers (e.g. facing, at side of, on) in:

     a) phrase 1 and,   b) phrase 2

Is there a difference in the relationships shown in the two phrases?

2) Describe the changes of speed you see. Why do you think the choreographer uses these?

3) Duo task – practical composition:

    Choose one of the following ideas:

        an argument – forbidden love – despondence

Discuss the meanings you wish to convey. Use at least three of the duo relationships you listed in 1) above as a basis for a short dance sequence.

═══════════

Activity C: refining the composition and practising performance of it.

Video snippet – as above – view as many times as required.

1) Watch how the dancers link their movements to make the phrases fluid and continuous.

   Watch also for the pauses.

   Make your own composition clear in its use of continuity and pauses and then practise it paying particular attention to continuity and pauses in conveying the meanings.

2) Watch the video again.
   Are the pauses dead still? If not, what keeps the dance movement going at these points?
   Practise your duo again working on the pauses to make them 'live and breathe'.

3) Have your duo videoed and then discuss with your partner ways in which your performance could be improved.
   Write a self-assessment on the composition and on your own performance in the duo.

───────

1) Questions in Activity A demand that the students study the time design, understand how it has been constructed (see *Methods of Construction 4)*, and consider how it contributes to the expression of the ideas that they think the snippet conveys.

2) In Activity B the students' perceptions are directed towards the content and the kinds of meanings it conveys to them. They would be expected to employ the terminology used to describe spatial and relationship aspects in the first activity and qualitative aspects of speed in the second (see *Section 1* and *Section 3*). In discerning the differences in the two phrases, they would be expected to note repetitions, developments and contrasts apparent in the content (see *Methods of Construction 5*).

3) In Activity C, an appreciation of the qualities of continuity and stillness as important elements is applied to their own work to improve performance in presenting meaning in dance.

The worksheet approach is further exemplified in Section 3.

– *Appreciation of Dance – a Theatre Visit* –

(for students 14–18)

BEFORE GOING TO SEE THE PERFORMANCE

Before going to a performance answer the following questions and do the following tasks. They have been designed to help you notice things about the performance you are going to see. Please note that there are no right or wrong answers and that more than one word could be listed in those questions that ask you to do this.

1) There are some words or concepts that can help us understand better the type of dance we are watching. Certain words seem to describe certain situations. *Comic* and *dramatic* are easy to use. A *dance-drama* tells a story. *Pure dance* would have nothing to do with anything except the dance movements themselves. Some people call this *abstract* dance but abstract dance might also be based on the movement of birds or the colours in a spectrum, for example, or anything 'abstracted' from something else. (See Section 2. *Methods of Construction 1.*)

From the following labels, try to select that which suitably describes the situations below: *dramatic dance, dance-drama, abstract dance, comic dance, pure dance.*

Remember there are no right or wrong answers and that for some situations more than one label might be appropriate.

a) A dance work depicting the event of an earthquake.
b) A dance work with a movement theme of curves, circles and spirals.
c) A dance work which depicts the movement of the sea.
d) A dance work which is titled 'Concerto' and is inspired by music alone.
e) A dance work using a nonsense rhyme.
f) A dance work called 'Magnetism' which uses electronic music.

2) Dance movements always communicate something, i.e. ideas, feelings, events, characteristics. When we see dances and want to talk about them we need words to describe the expression in the movements.

Look at picture 11 on page 53. List any of the following words which seem to describe the expression in the movement.

Exhilaration, powerfulness, playfulness, energy, freedom, joy, strength.

3) We need words also to describe the particular qualities we can see in a movement.

Which of the following words would you use to describe the qualities in the movement:

buoyant, tense, graceful, strong, curved, flowing, delicate, angular.

4) Often it is the shape or line created in the space that makes us notice a movement.

Look at picture 9 on page 53.

a) Can you find curves, straight lines, and angles created by the pair?
b) What shape are the spaces created by the dancers' limbs?
c) What shape in space does the duo create?

5) Now that we have some words, we can use them and others to describe dance movements.

In the following examples the choreographer is trying to express feelings.

a) Imagine a dance which expresses gaiety, joyfulness and exhilaration. What sort of movements would the choreographer use to express this mood?
b) Think of another feeling, describe it and the sort of movements you might expect in a dance which depicts it.

6) When we talk about dance works we need to refer to other aspects besides the movement, i.e. the sound accompaniment, the design of the set, the lighting, the props, the make-up and costumes.

a) In a small group discuss the role of each of these aspects in a dance work that you have seen recently.
b) Write notes on each aspect and how it contributed to the expression/meaning in the dance.

Now see the performance. Enjoy it and trust your own feelings about it.

AFTER THE PERFORMANCE

After the performance answer the following questions and do the following tasks in relation to the dance work you saw. (If there was more than one work choose the one you liked best.)

1) Your programme can give you a lot of information. Use it to answer the following.

a) What dance work did you see?
b Who choreographed it and when was it first produced?
c) Name the designer and briefly describe the set, the lighting, and the costumes.
d) Who composed the music and what sort was it (e.g. electronic, jazz, vocal sound, classical)?

2) You will soon be writing a review of the dance work. To help you, let's first make some more observations.

a) What type of dance work was it (dance-drama, pure dance, abstract, etc.)? Perhaps it was a combination of two or more types.
b) What was the style of the work (e.g. classical, jazz, folk, modern)?
c) Name two of the dancers and write a few sentences about their performances.

3) The meaning of the dance work is not something that is predetermined, but is entirely up to you, the member of the audience. Of course, the dance may not be 'about' anything at all.

a) What do you think were the main ideas or feelings expressed in the dance work by the choreographer?
b) How did it make *you* feel?
c) Try to remember which movements you think most expressed the ideas or feelings contained in the dance. Describe two of these movements and say why you think they most expressed the ideas or feelings.

4) Closely observing the dance work takes practice.

a) List any of the following that you noticed about the dance. You can add your own observations to those below.

* An important pattern of movement was repeated several times.

* Movement in unison was used.

* Sometimes the dancers did the same movements one after the other.

* There was a lot of variety in the movement content of the dance work.

* The patterns and shapes the dancers made were interesting and varied.

* All the various parts or sections of the dance seemed to fit together well.

b) Can you make a list of words to describe qualities of movement in the dance work? If you consider the work to consist of different sections, how do the words for one section compare with those for another?

c) Visualise a particularly exciting or memorable moment from the dance. Can you make a drawing of it?

5) You are now quite ready to write a review of the dance work. Look through your own work from before the performance and afterwards and make sure that in your review you consider all the aspects, i.e. choreography, set design, lighting, costumes, etc.

Informed members of the public are just as important to dance as dancers.

– *Presentation of Dance to an Audience* –

ALIGNMENT: OBSERVING AND STRUCTURING MOVEMENT INTO ADVANTAGEOUS ALIGNMENT

1) Presented with a phrase of continuous movement emphasising pattern in space, the student-composer should observe it and:
a) correct the alignment of the body in relation to the front during any of the movements which are lost to the audience, and

b) find about 4–6 stopping places within the phrase which shows pleasing alignment in relation to an audience.

2) Have the dancer repeat the continuous movement phrase until the corrections in a) above have been mastered.

3) Have the dancer repeat the phrase with the agreed stops and make sure that an audience could appreciate the spatial patterns in movement and the body shapes in stillness. Define also, the nature of the stillness, whether breath moments which seem to continue in movement often through line, or, absolute and held stillness. The latter require perfect alignment.

Reference: Section 2. *Methods of Construction 2*

There is no set criterion for good alignment but the following guidelines might be helpful:

a) avoid using the forward and backward directions in gestures when facing the front or back. These lines are better placed sideways or diagonally in relation to an audience.
b) Try to get the performer to *feel* a sense of line throughout the body, e.g. an open diagonal line from high-right to deep-left requires a tilt from the waist so that the line passes through and beyond the shoulders in a straight line.
c) The positioning of body parts to give the maximum effect to body shape needs to be carefully analysed in an aesthetic way. Just as in a photograph, a small tilt of the head could make all the difference to the total body shape and its meaning.
d) If the moments of stillness are required to 'live on', try to get the performer to achieve a sense of movement through and beyond the lines and curves the body is making. Then the audience may momentarily visually extend these lines or curves from the dancer's extremities on into space.

– *Presentation of Dance to an Audience* –

OBSERVATION OF RELATIONSHIP

1) Two observers watch eight dancers. Each dancer should compose a short sequence using a spatial form based on a picture.

2) Each of the observers should select two dancers whose sequences seem to complement each other.

3) Keep the sequences as composed but by means of spatial placing, timing and pausing, create an illusion of duo relationship.

Reference: Section 2. *Methods of Construction 3*

1) The observer could look for some of the following features:
   a) repetition of design in the two bodies,
   b) repetition of air pathways,
   c) repetition in direction,
   d) complementing action,
   e) contrast in levels.

2) When the duo relationship is made it might appear harmonious and related like a two-part song.

3) The observer should work from one front and concentrate upon the visual design created by the two bodies.

– *Presentation of Dance to an Audience* –

OBSERVATION OF RELATIONSHIP

1) Select *one* of the following ideas:
   a) Peace and Sympathy
   b) Streetwise – Gamins
   c) Workers
   d) Growing Excitement
   e) Or any other scene-setting situation (perhaps an opening to a dance-drama)

2) Have six couples compose short duo sequences.

3) The composer/observer could then manipulate the six couple sequences, by means of spatial placing, timing and pausing, into a group of related couples. He/she could look for matching and complementary movement and use these parts of the sequences simultaneously. He/she should aim to use stillness at different times for each couple and avoid having more than three couples moving at the same time unless the movements are the same or very complementary.

4) Since each couple will be doing something different the above structure of their relationship should aim for unity. To reinforce the unity, it might then be appropriate to create a transition to be performed in unison before the group dance ends or goes on to another section.

It is essential that the composer/observer works from the front. He/she can then aim to focus the attention on the various moving parts of the group in interesting ways. For instance, this could be effected by having a couple towards the centre-back start, and then a front corner couple complementing their action a moment later. There are endless ways of initiating, interrupting and linking moments of each of the couples' sequences and the composer should constantly stand back to evaluate the effect.

– *Composition and Evaluation* –

WITH A GROUP OF 7

1) Discover appropriate numerical variations, group shapes and spatial (as if in photographs) placings to express one of the following:
a) Children's Games
b) Villagers Mourning War Victims
c) Dictators and Oppressed
d Cardboard City

2) Form a dance using some of the discovered group shapes and spatial placings.

3) After completion attempt to evaluate the dance in terms of the principles of balance and proportion.

Reference: Section 2. *Methods of Construction 3 and 5*

Numerical relationship should be varied as much as possible. The area defined for the dance should be used to the fullest extent, with the groups placed in a variety of places within the area and in different relationship with each other. The use of props or rostra could enhance the presentation.

– *Composition and Evaluation* –

1) Compose a dance.
2) Report in writing on the emergence of the idea/motivation and why the stimulus was chosen. Describe the form of the composition and give details of the material content with reasons for its choice.

Reference: Section 2

– *Composition Problems* –

Assignments for more advanced students suitable for exploration, written report and group discussion.

1) a) Make an action phrase.
   b) Manipulate it to make it comic in two different ways.
   c) Demonstrate and explain how this has been achieved.
   c) Find general principles which arise out of the work.

2) a) Make a phrase of movement for two people which shows them to be very dramatically involved with each other.
   b) Discover ways of keeping this involvement yet projecting it to the audience.
   c) Detail possible answers to the problem of projection of dramatic involvement.

3) a) With a group of six find and demonstrate as many numerical relationships, placement relationships and group shapes as possible.
   b) Present views on the expressive connotations implicit in them.

4) a) Make simple dance phrases to express i) sorrow ii) excitement.
   b) Make both the phrases dramatic.
   c) Explain how the movement was dramatised.

5) a) Find several representational movements which suggest: i) an old aged character ii) a group of gossips.
   b) Make two phrases of symbolic movement utilising the above.
   c) Explain how representation of the characters was retained without the use of mime.

6) a) Make two simple dance phrases based on a non-European dance style (e.g. South Asian, Afro-Caribbean) – abstracting the essence of the style.
   b) Use the two phrases as motifs for a dance based upon a story or custom of the place of origin.
   c) Explain how the motifs were adapted/extended to tell the story and how the style was defined.

REFERENCES

Banes S. (1980) *Terpsichore in Sneakers – Post Modern Dance*, Houghton Mifflin Co.

Banes S. (1987) Second Edition

Best D. (1985) *Feeling and Reason in the Arts*, Allen and Unwin

Burnside F. (1994) 'Matthew Bourne and Kim Brandstrup' in *Dance Theatre Journal Vol. 11 No. 2*, Spring/Summer 1994

Curl G. (1973) Lecture on Aesthetic Judgements in Dance in *Collected Conference Papers in Dance* – A.T.C.D.E.

Dewey J. (1946) *The Public and its Problems*, Gateway Books

Foster S.L. (1986) *Reading Dancing – Bodies and Subjects in Contemporary American Dance*, University of California Press

Fraleigh S.H. (1987) *Dance and the Lived Body – A Descriptive Aesthetics*, University of Pittsburgh Press

Hayes E.R. (1955) *Dance Composition and Production for High Schools and Colleges*, The Ronald Press

H'Doubler M.N. (1957) *Dance: A Creative Art Experience*, University of Wisconsin Press

Jordan S. (1992) *Striding Out – Aspects of Contemporary and New Dance in Britain*, Dance Books

Jowitt D. (1988) *Time and the Dancing Image*, University of California Press

Laban R. (1948) *Modern Educational Dance*, Macdonald & Evans

Laban, R. (1960) *The Mastery of Movement*, second edition revised by L. Ullmann, Macdonald & Evans

Langer S. (1953) *Feeling and Form*, Routledge & Kegan Paul

Mackrell J. (1992) *Out of Line – The Story of British New Dance*, Dance Books

Martin J. (1933) *The Modern Dance*, Dance Horizons Inc.

Matheson K. (1992) 'Breaking Boundaries' in *Dance as a Theatre Art*, Cohen S.J. (ed), Princeton Book Co. Publishers

Osborne H. (1968) *Aesthetics and Art Theory. An Historical Introduction*, Longmans, Green

Preston-Dunlop V. (1963) *A Handbook for Modern Educational Dance*, Macdonald & Evans

Read H. (1931) *The Meaning of Art*, Penguin

Redfern H.B. (1973) *Concepts in Modern Educational Dance*, Henry Kimpton

Reid A.L. (1969) Lecture on Aesthetics and Education. Conference

Report, Association of Principals of Women's Colleges of Physical Education

Robertson A. and Hutera D. (1988) *The Dance Handbook*, Longman Group UK.

Rolfe L. and Harlow M. (1997) *Let's Look at Dance*, David Fulton Publishers

Roy Sanjoy (ed.) (1999) *White Man Sleeps – Creative Insights*, Dance Books Ltd.

Rubidge S. (1991) 'Lives of the great poisoners' in *Dance Theatre Journal Vol. 8. No. 4*, Spring 1991

Seigel M. (1979) *The Shapes of Change*, Avon Books

Servos N. (1984) *Pina Bausch-Wuppertal Dance Theatre or the Art of Training a Goldfish*, trans. P. Stadie, Ballett Buhnen Verlag

Smith-Autard J.M. and Schofield J. (1995) Resource-based Teaching and Interactive Video in *Proceedings of Conference, 'Border Tensions'*, University of Surrey

Smith-Autard J.M. and Schofield J. (1995) Developments in Dance Pedagogy through Application of Multimedia in Interactive Video in *Proceedings of Dance '95 – Move into the Future*, Conference at Bretton Hall College, Yorkshire

Smith-Autard J.M. and Schofield J. (1997) Nine lectures in *Workshop in Multimedia and Dance Pedagogy – Developing Expertise* Proceedings of Conference at the University of Limerick, Ireland

Smith J.M. and Newman S. (1978) *Dance Appreciation Teaching Units for Schools and Colleges*, Ballet Rambert and Thames Polytechnic

Smith-Autard J.M. (1994) *The Art of Dance in Education*, A & C Black

Video and CD Resources

BBC Educational Publishing *Sportsbank Special: Dance*. Video pack of 150 minutes – programmes produced by Sarah Miller, a music CD and a book for teachers written by Smith-Autard J.M. (1998)

Bedford Interactive Productions Ltd. in collaboration with the Ludus Dance Company, *Wild Child CD Resource Pack* (1999). See Section 3 of this book for details of content

Bruce C. (1984) *Intimate Pages* and (1986) *Sergeant Early's Dream* on *Evening with the Ballet Rambert Company*, Virgin Classics, VVD 346 VHS (1986)

Kylian J. (1984) *L'Enfant et les Sortilèges*, Netherlands Dans Theater, produced by Virgin Video, VVD 382 (1986)

North, R. (1984) *Lonely Town, Lonely Street* on *An Evening with the Ballet Rambert Company*, Virgin Classics, VVD 346 VHS (1986)

Siobhan Davies Dance Company, *White Man Sleeps, Wyoming*, London, Dance Videos, DV15 (1998)

CONTACT
INFORMATION

Bedford Interactive Productions Ltd.
19 Edge Road, Thornhill,
Dewsbury, West Yorkshire
WF12 0QA UK.

Tel: 01924 464049
Fax: 01924 485898
Email: JSmithAutard@compuserve.com

INDEX